6 95

ACTS

Charles H. Talbert

KNOX PREACHING GUIDES
John H. Hayes, Editor

John Knox Press
ATLANTA

To
the Baptist Churches of
Marion Junction, Alabama
and
Little Mount, Kentucky

Library of Congress Cataloging in Publication Data

Talbert, Charles H.
  Acts.

  (Knox preaching guides)
  Bibliography: p.
  1. Bible. N.T. Acts—Commentaries. 2. Bible. N.T.
Acts—Homiletical use. I. Title. II. Series.
BS2625.3.T35 1985   226'.606   84-12536
ISBN 0-8042-3231-8

Contents

ACTS

Introduction

What Is Acts?

Although the Acts of the Apostles in our New Testaments functions as a bridge between the four gospels and the Pauline epistles, originally it was volume two of a work of which the Gospel of Luke was volume one. Does Luke-Acts belong to any literary genre or type of literature known in antiquity? Until recently, critical orthodoxy's answer had been a negative. All of the canonical gospels were regarded as literarily, as well as theologically, *sui generis*. In recent times, there has been a recognition that an absolutely unique literary form would not have been intelligible to its readers. Hence there has been an effort to locate the gospels, including Luke-Acts, within their proper literary milieu in Mediterranean antiquity. Various options have been proposed both from the Jewish and from the Greco-Roman environments of early Christianity. The alternative that has seemed most convincing to me for Luke-Acts is the one suggested years ago by Hermann von Soden. Luke-Acts is similar to the biographies of certain founders of philosophical schools that contained within themselves not only the life of the founder (what we will call *a*) but also a list or brief narrative of his successors and selected other disciples (what we will call *b*).

Charting the trajectory of this type of biographical writing is helpful in our grasping the place of Luke-Acts within this sub-genre of biography and its role in early Christianity. (1)

The earliest evidence, to my knowledge, we have for the plan of Luke-Acts (what I call the *a* plus *b* form; see below) is in a pre-Christian biography of Aristotle. Here the life of Aristotle is followed by a succession list. (2) In Diogenes Laertius certain lives of philosophers reflect this pattern. In some of them not only is there a life of the founder, (*a*), followed by a brief narrative of his successors and selected other disciples, (*b*), but also an extensive statement of the teachings of the philosopher, (*c*). Examination of Laertius' references to the sources for his lives shows that the material in the (*c*) component comes from a different origin than that in (*a* plus *b*). This allows one to conclude that in his *Lives of the Philosophers* Laertius took over individual biographies of some founders that were written in terms of an (*a*) plus (*b*) pattern and added the (*c*) component himself. Either he or his sources sometimes filled out the (*b*) component with anecdotes and sayings of the founder's successors so that (*b*) is not a list but a brief narrative. (3) In the *Life of Pachomius* we find a Christian appropriation of this sub-genre of ancient biography. It is fitting because this biography deals with both the father of coenobitic monasticism and his successors in the community. The early part of the biography deals with the career of Pachomius. In section 117, in language that may be regarded as the technical terminology of succession characteristic of the philosophical schools, he appoints Orsisius to succeed him. In the sections that follow we are told what Orsisius did and said (118–129), zealously emulating the life of Pachomius (119). Then Orsisius appoints Theodore (130). In the chapters that follow we are told what Theodore did and said. This biography confirms not only that such biographical forms existed well into our era but also that when appropriate there was no obstacle to Christian appropriation of this sub-genre of biography.

When one has charted the development of the (*a*) plus (*b*) biographical pattern from pre-Christian times to its later Christian appropriation, certain things are obvious. (1) The sub-genre has a long life. (2) It is appropriate only where the hero is a founder of a community (e.g., philosophical school or monastery) whose death demands successors. (3) The material about the successors can be given briefly in a list or more extensively in a narrative. The narrative tends to expand in length over the lifetime of the sub-genre. It is longer in Christian circles than in non-Christian ones. (4) In the second component, (*b*), when a narrative is given, the emphasis is on the successor(s) emulating the founder.

Luke-Acts tells the story of the life of Jesus in such a way that he is depicted as the founder of the Christian community who provides for its continuation after his departure. The narrative about the community led by his appointed ones portrays the Twelve and Paul in such a way that they reproduce in their careers the prototypical events of the career of the earthly Jesus. The (*b*) component is long, longer even than that in the *Life of Pachomius*. It is expanded with novelistic elements throughout (e.g., the sea journey). Nevertheless, Acts remains within the general bounds of an (*a*) plus (*b*) biography within antiquity, both in terms of its pattern and in terms of its function.

How Should Acts Be Read?

In the past Acts has been studied in relation to the Pauline epistles and Luke has been read in connection with the other two Synoptic gospels, usually in a gospel parallels. This procedure reflects an approach to Luke-Acts that is concerned primarily with historical questions. Luke is used as a potential source for the reconstruction of the life of the historical Jesus, while Acts is mined for historical data that may assist us in writing the history of early Christianity. While this approach is legitimate for the historian, it is not the way to read Luke-Acts that is most beneficial to the preacher.

The impact of literary criticism on redaction criticism in this country has led to a different way of reading the Lukan writings. The gospel is read in relation to Acts and Acts in relation to Luke. Each is regarded as a commentary on the other. The object in reading the two volumes is to enter into the narrative world of the text and listen to what Luke-Acts wants to say about religious reality. It is the Lukan theological point of view that is sought. When read in this way, Luke-Acts represents a theological perspective alongside that of Paul, the Fourth Gospel, and other New Testament theologians. Since it was Luke and Acts in their present form that were deemed canonical by the early church, it is this way of reading the Lukan narrative that seems most in line with the

canonical intent. It is this way of reading Acts that will be
followed in this book. Given this approach to Acts, the best
companion volume to this one in an attempt to understand
the Lukan point of view is my book, *Reading Luke: A Literary
and Theological Commentary on the Third Gospel* (New York:
Crossroad, 1982).

Is Acts a Proper Text from Which to Preach?

There is little doubt about the value of the canonical gospels or of the major Pauline letters for preaching. Acts is another matter. It is a narrative more about the church than
about Christ. This raises the question to what extent information about the Christian churches was used as a part of
early Christian preaching and teaching.

Early Christian proclamation focused not only on the story
of Jesus and its significance but also on the experience of early Christians. This is true both in Paul's time and a generation later in the time of Luke-Acts.

(1) Jacob Jervell, *Luke and the People of God* (Minneapolis:
Augsburg, 1972), pp. 19–39, has argued that conditions in the
early church were favorable for the formation of a tradition
about apostolic times. This was so because various practical
motives led to its preservation. Reports of the establishment
of a congregation played a role in missionary proclamation
(e.g., Rom 1:8; 1 Thess 1:8–10; 2 Cor 3:1–3). Boasting about a
congregation's faith and steadfastness in affliction functions
as consolation to others (2 Thess 1:4; 1 Thess 3:6). Reports
about congregations function parenetically (2 Cor 8:1–7;
9:1–5; 1 Thess 1:6–10). Reports about an apostle function
parenetically (2 Thess 3:7–13; Phil 3:17; 4:9; 1 Cor 4:17;
11:1). The kerygma summarized in 1 Cor 15:3–11 contained
within itself a tradition about the apostles and the congregations. All of these pieces of information from the Pauline letters show that information about the churches and the
apostles functioned as material for preaching and teaching in
the early church.

(2) It is also true that the Third Evangelist believed that
the experience of disciples was fit material for proclamation.
In Luke 8:39, Jesus tells the cured demoniac who wanted to
be with him to return home, "and declare how much God has
done for you." The man went away, "proclaiming ... how

much Jesus had done for him." It was the man's experience that was the content of his proclamation. This was so because Jesus had commanded him to do it. In Acts 26:16, moreover, the risen Lord tells Paul: "I have appeared to you for this purpose, to appoint you to serve and bear witness to the things in which you have seen me and to those in which I will appear to you." Again the Lord commands proclamation to be about Paul's own experience. Whether, then, it was the Christians of the fifties or those at the end of the first century, the conviction was the same. Proclamation focuses not only on the story of Jesus and theological statements about the significance of the Christ-event but also on the experience of the early Christians and their apostles. Tradition and testimony hang together. If this was so, then it helps explain why the canon contains a narrative about the early church's history. This too was legitimate material for preaching and teaching. If it was so for them, it may be so for us. On this assumption, the following pages are based.

The Commission:
A Mission to Do
(Acts 1:1–14)

Acts 1:1–14 constitutes a coherent unit of thought consisting of three parts, each of which makes a distinct point or points. (1) The first part, vss. 1–3, is a secondary preface (see Luke 1:1–4 for the primary preface) like those found in Diodorus Siculus II:1 and III:1 on the one hand and in Josephus, *Antiquities*, Books 8 and 13 on the other, where books begin with summaries of what has preceded but not what lies ahead. This secondary preface in Acts is shaped so as to say two things related to the overall unit, vss. 1–14: (a) Jesus ascended after giving instructions to his chosen apostles (vs. 2—see Luke 6:12–16); and (b) this instruction was "through forty days" (vs. 3). The reference to the forty days is "new" in the Lukan narrative. It is not found in Luke 24 which seems to put resurrection, appearances, and ascension all on one long day. Its purpose here is to say that the apostles (vs. 2b), like Moses who was forty days on the mountain (Exod 24:12–18) or Baruch who was forty days receiving his revelation (2 Baruch 76:1–4), are fully instructed. For a similar concern of the author of Acts, note Acts 20:20, 27, 31 where the Lukan Paul's interest is in the full instruction of the Ephesian elders.

(2) The second part, vss. 4–11, gives the reader two illustrations of the post-resurrection instruction of the apostles. The two pericopes (vss. 4–8; 9–11) are formally similar. On the one hand, vss. 4–8 consist of (a) the risen Jesus' word (vss. 4–5—see Luke 24:49) not to depart from Jerusalem until they have experienced the promised baptism in the Holy Spirit (see Isa 32:15; Joel 2:28–29); (b) the disciples' query (vs. 6): "Lord, will you at this time restore the kingdom to Israel?" (Luke 19:11; see Jer 23:1–8; Ezek 17; 34; Sirach 36:1–17, for the restoration of Israel at the End time); (c) the risen Jesus' response in two parts (vss. 7–8): first, a reproof (vs. 7—see Luke 17:20; Mark 13:32): "It is not for you to know the times or seasons which the Father has fixed by his own authority";

second, a promise (vs. 8—see Luke 24:47–48): "But you shall receive power when the Holy Spirit has come upon you; and you shall be my witnesses in Jerusalem and in all Judea and Samaria and to the end of the earth" (Isa 49:6; Psalms of Solomon 8:15).

On the other hand, vss. 9–11 consist of similar components: (a) the risen Jesus' action (vs. 9—Luke 24:51), being taken up into heaven; (b) the disciples' behavior (vs. 10a), gazing into heaven; (c) the angelic response (vss. 10b–11): first, a reproof (vs. 11a)—"Men of Galilee, why do you stand looking into heaven?"; second, a promise (vs. 11b)—"This Jesus, who was taken up from you into heaven, will come in the same way as you saw him go into heaven" (see Luke 18:1–8).

The first of these instructional pericopes reproves apocalyptic enthusiasm (that is, the attempt to calculate the time of the End of the world) and promises instead an empowering for mission. The second reproves wistful, defeated quietism and promises the certainty of Jesus' second coming.

(3) The third part, vss. 12–14, sets out the exemplary behavior of those who are fully instructed. *They pray!* The reference to the united prayer of the disciples must be understood in terms of the context, both the immediate context of Acts 1:1–14 and the larger context of Luke-Acts as a whole. The immediate context with its focus on the two illustrations of post-resurrection instruction of the apostles enables us to see the import of the prayer as twofold. On the one hand, they are praying for the promise of the Father (vss. 4–5), the coming of the Holy Spirit which will empower them for their witness (vs. 8). In so doing they are acting in obedience to the words of the pre-Easter Jesus in Luke 11:9–13: "Ask, and it will be given you . . . the heavenly Father (will) give the Holy Spirit to those who ask him!" On the other hand, they are praying for the coming of the Son of Man, "this Jesus, who . . . will come in the same way as you saw him go into heaven" (vs. 11). In so doing they are acting in accord with the pre-Easter Jesus' words in Luke 18:1–8 where in the parable of the unjust judge he told them "they ought always to pray and not lose heart" (vs. 1) because God will "vindicate his elect, who cry to him day and night" (vs. 7a—see Rev 6:9–11).

This third part of Acts 1:1–14 shows the apostles acting in a way that reflects the Evangelist's conception of how Jesus taught them to behave in just such a situation as they find themselves: waiting for God to act. (a) If you want the empowering of the Holy Spirit, pray. (b) If you want the parousia of Jesus, pray. In any case, while you wait, pray!

This thought unit can be preached in a number of ways. Two will be mentioned here. One possibility would be a sermon on "Creative Waiting." The OT speaks frequently about waiting for God to act (for example, Pss 27:14; 37:34; 130:5; Isa 8:17; Micah 7:7) and promises benefits to those who do wait on God (Isa 40:31). In this passage in Acts the disciples are depicted as in a period of waiting. They are waiting for their empowering; they also await their vindication at the parousia. The Lukan message is that a creative use of a waiting period is to pray. Pray for empowering and for the parousia.

Another option for a sermon based on this passage would be "A Mission to Do." The introduction would pose the issue. When the risen Jesus faced his departure from those with whom he had lived so closely during his earthly life, what was uppermost in his mind? As in the case of the First Gospel (Matt 28:19–20), the Lukan Evangelist has the risen Jesus concerned about the *mission* to be carried out by his disciples after his departure and this mission and its nature should form the two foci for preaching on this text. The call to mission is given in Acts 1:8b (see Luke 24:46–48). The disciples are presented with a two-fold charge. The first stresses the object of witness—"of me"—while the second focuses on the geography of witness—"to the ends of the earth." The prerequisite for mission is the power of the Holy Spirit (Acts 1:4–5, 8a; Luke 24:49). The ones addressed are those who had been with Jesus throughout his earthly life. They know the facts. What they lack is the experience of the empowering presence of God (Acts 1:21–22). They are to act according to a timetable supplied by the risen Lord. They are not to move out until they have had the necessary experience (Acts 1:8; Luke 24:48–49; 5:1–11). If the call is to be carried out effectively, certain distractions from mission must be overcome. As did the risen Jesus, preoccupation with the time of the End must be rejected as a distraction (Acts 1:6–7). Buttressed by the angelic promise, loss of confidence about the meaningfulness of history must be remedied (1:9–11). When the Third Evangelist says that the risen Jesus will come again as his disciples saw him go, he refers to Jesus' going in a cloud (i.e., in the presence of God). So it is the Lukan belief that he will come again in a cloud (Luke 21:27—"you will see the Son of Man coming in a cloud with power and great glory"). This is Luke's way of saying that all of history moves to the vindication of Jesus and what he stands for. That he departs or has departed does not undermine Christian confidence in the ultimate outcome of history. In Jesus' ascension Christians have a preview of the End of history. The prelude to mission, in the Lukan view, is prayer (Acts 1:12–14; see Luke 11:13). The conclusion to the sermon would need to pull together the various strands of the text. Just before the Lukan Jesus departed to the Father, he gave his disciples a mission to do. He made it clear, however, that this mission could not proceed until those who knew the facts about his life came to know God experientially. The disciples were not to be distracted from this mission and its prior empowering. If they were to be empowered, moreover, they were to pray.

The Commission Fulfilled: Stage One
(Acts 1:15—12:24)

Finding Laborers for the Harvest (1:15–26)

Acts 1:15–26 is a thought unit distinct from 1:1–14, yet related to the former. In 1:1–14 the concern is that the witnesses be empowered and ultimately vindicated; in 1:15–26 it is that the number of the witnesses be complete. The twelve apostles are said to possess a ministry (*diakonia*, vs. 17) and apostleship (vs. 25) which involve being a witness to Jesus' resurrection (vs. 22b). The Lukan view is that after the resurrection of Jesus this new evidence is presented to Israel by the Twelve (Acts 5:32; 10:39–42; 13:31) in an effort to overcome the ignorance that produced Jesus' death (Acts 3:17) and to gain Jewish repentance (Acts 2:38; 3:19). This mission to Israel is foreshadowed in Luke 9:1–6 where the Twelve are sent out by Jesus. Their crucial role in relation to Israel is indicated by Luke 22:28–30 where it is said that they will sit on thrones judging the twelve tribes. In order for the witnesses to be effective, they must not only be empowered (Acts 1:8, 4–5) but also their symbolic number must be complete. Prophetic symbolism demands twelve witnesses for the twelve tribes. (Prophetic symbolism continued in the Christian community depicted by Acts—see, for example, 21:10–11). Acts 1:15–26, therefore, just as Acts 1:1–14, is concerned with preparation for the Mission that is about to begin. (The Twelve perform two main functions in Luke-Acts. They are both witnesses to Israel and they are guarantors of the True tradition of Jesus [compare Luke 1:2 with Acts 1:21–22]. Neither can be eliminated. In this passage, however, the major emphasis is on their mission to Israel.)

In terms of its surface structure, Acts 1:15–26 consists of (1) an introduction (vs. 15), (2) Peter's speech (vss. 16–22), and (3) the response to Peter's speech (vss. 23–26). Each of these components will be examined in turn.

(1) Vs. 15 is the introduction to the entire unit. To say "the

company of persons was in all about a hundred and twenty"
is important in at least two ways. First, since according to
Jewish law 120 was the number of men required to establish
a community with its own Council, the reference indicates
that the disciples were a group of sufficient size to constitute
a new community. Second, the number 120 is symbolic,
probably referring to the restored tribes of Israel. To summa-
rize: the 120 disciples, symbolizing the restored Israel (Acts
15:16), are of sufficient size to require a council of leaders for
themselves. This indicates the legitimacy, according to Jewish law, of the action that is to follow. From the first, then,
we are confronted with the faithfulness to Judaism of the disciples. This necessary leadership, as we will see in the next
component of the unit, is now incomplete.

(2) Vss. 16–22 comprise a speech of Peter. The speech falls
into two parts (vss. 16–20; 21–22), each introduced by the vo-
cabulary of divine necessity: *"it was necessary (edei*—vs. 16)
for scripture to be fulfilled concerning Judas"*; "it is necessary*
(*dei*—vs. 21) that one of the men accompanying us become
with us a witness." The first part of the speech tells why the
number of the Twelve is incomplete. Judas' defection was
necessary in order to fulfill Scripture. Judas' defection is described in an ABA' pattern in vss. 16b–19:

A—Judas was guide to those who arrested Jesus (vs. 16b)
   B—Judas was allocated his share in this ministry
   (vs. 17)
A'—Judas was not able to enjoy the reward of his wickedness (see Luke 22:3–6) but rather died, leaving his
   field untended (vss. 18–19).

The pattern makes the point that although Judas was num-
bered among the Twelve (vs. 17—see Luke 6:12–16), his
treachery left a vacancy in the group (see Luke 24:33—the
Eleven).

These points are fulfillments of Scripture. The A and A'
parts of the pattern fulfill Ps 69:25 (LXX): "Let his habitation
become desolate, and let there be no one to live in it." This is
taken to refer to the fact that Judas' death prevented his caring for his land. The B part of the pattern fulfills Ps 109:8:
"His office (*episkopen*) let another take." This, of course, refers to the fact that the vacancy left by Judas' defection must

be filled by another. This defection, although a part of the divine plan, still requires a replacement.

The second part of the speech of Peter (vss. 21–22) speaks of the necessity of completing the number of the Twelve. A qualified replacement is needed. In contrast to Paul for whom the qualifications for apostleship included having seen the risen Lord (1 Cor 9:1, 15:8) and having received a call (Gal. 1:15–16), Luke-Acts regards an apostle's qualifications to include, in addition, having accompanied Jesus from the baptism of John to the ascension. There was apparently a pool of possibilities from which to choose (see Luke 24:9, "all the rest"; 24:33, "those with the apostles"). Such a qualified person "must become with us a witness to his resurrection" (vs. 22b).

(3) Vss. 23–26 constitute the response to Peter's speech. The pattern of the unit is ABA'.

A—Narration (vs. 23): "And they put forward"
   B—Prayer (vss. 24–25): "And they said"
A'—Narration (vs. 26): "And they gave"; "And it fell";
                    "And he was enrolled."

In this section we observe the procedure of the action to replace Judas. Two qualified people are put forward. In prayer the Lord (the risen Jesus—see Acts 1:2) is asked to make the choice because he knows the hearts of men (see 1 Sam 16:7). In this the disciples are following the word of the Lukan Jesus (Luke 10:2). They are also acting in a way that will be characteristic of the later church in Acts (e.g., 1:14; 4:31; 9:11; 10:2, 9; 12:5; 13:3, etc.). Their prayer is answered and Matthias is enrolled with the Eleven. The number of the Twelve is now complete. What remains of the preparations for the upcoming Mission is their empowering, which will be taken care of in Acts 2.

This passage may serve as the text for a sermon, "Finding Laborers for the Harvest." The introduction would pose the problem. How does the church go about finding sufficient numbers of qualified laborers for the harvest? It is this problem and its solution that are addressed by Acts 1:15–26. The need is defined in a speech by Peter in vss. 16–22. The reason behind the need is the incomplete number of the witnesses (vss. 16–20). The nature of the need is twofold. First, the witness must be a qualified person (vss. 21–22). Second, the person must be chosen by the Lord (vs. 24). How the need is met is depicted by means of a prayer and its answer (vss. 23–26). The prayer comes in verses 24–25. Luke 10:2 has the Lukan Jesus say: "The harvest is plentiful, but the laborers are few; pray therefore the Lord of the harvest to send out laborers into his harvest." Acts 1:25–25 portrays the early disciples in the exemplary posture of prayer for this very objective (cf. Acts 13:1–3 for a similar motif). The prayer's answer is narrated in verses 23 and 26. That the Lord answered is not surprising given Jesus' teaching about God's willingness to answer prayer (Luke 11:5–10). In conclusion one must note that the two halves of Acts each begin with the choice of witnesses for the Mission at hand and ahead (1:15–26 completing the action begun in Luke 6:12–16; Acts 9:1–30 and 13:1–3). The Lord supplies what is needed before the Mission is launched. His disciples' role is to pray that the Lord of the harvest will supply the needed laborers.

Empowering and Its Effects (2:1–47)

Acts 2:1–47 tells of events that occurred on the day of Pentecost (vs. 1). Pentecost in the OT was called the Feast of Weeks (Exod 23:16; Lev 23:15–21; Deut 16:9–12). It was a one day festival celebrating the wheat harvest. In the pseudepigraphical book of Jubilees, Chapter 6, the festival is associated with the renewal of the covenant made with Noah and then with Moses. In fact, in Jubilees all the covenants were made on the day of Pentecost. For the Covenanters of Qumran (the members of the Dead Sea Scrolls community), Pentecost was the day when they made the annual renewal of the oath which they took when they entered the community. At least by the second century A.D. rabbinic Judaism regarded Pentecost as the day the law was given at Sinai. The narrative of Acts 2 seems to understand the Christian Pentecost in terms of the events that took place at Sinai. The new convenant (see Luke 22:20) has its counterpart to the Sinai theophany of the Old Covenant. As in Jubilees, these covenantal occurrences are linked with the Feast of Pentecost.

The surface structure of Acts 2:1–47 falls into four parts: (1) a narrative (vss. 1–11) describing the Pentecostal phenomena; (2) speeches giving the meaning of the phenomena (vss. 12–36); (3) a dialogue (vss. 37–40) explaining the proper re-

sponse to the phenomena and their interpretation; and (4) a
narrative (vss. 41–47) telling of the results of the Pentecostal
events and their interpretation. We may turn to an examination of each of these components.

(1) The narrative of 2:1–11 tells about the Pentecostal phenomena in terms that both are characteristically Lukan and
echo the events of the Sinai theophany in the OT. On the one
hand, any intrusion of the heavenly world into human affairs
in Luke-Acts is likely to be accompanied by visions and audi-
tions (e.g., Luke 1:11, 13–17; 2:9, 10–11; 3:21–22; 9:30–31;
22:43; 24:4–7; Acts 9:3, 4–6; 10:3–6, 10–15; 12:7–8; 16:9–10;
18:9–10; 23:11; 27:23–24), that is, things seen and things
heard. It is certainly the case in Acts 2. Likewise in Luke-Acts
most happenings are fulfillments of some kind of prophecy
(see Luke 1:1—"a narrative of the things which have been
fulfilled among us"). So here the prophecy of John the Baptist ("he will baptize you with the Holy Spirit and with
fire"—Luke 3:16) is fulfilled. Also the prophecies of Jesus
("And behold, I send the promise of my Father upon you"—
Luke 24:49; "before many days you shall be baptized with
the Holy Spirit"—Acts 1:5; "But you shall receive power after the Holy Spirit has come upon you"—Acts 1:8) are fulfilled at Pentecost. Much that is characteristically Lukan is
found in Acts 2:1–11.

On the other hand, a number of the features of the narrative echo the Sinai events. The sound from heaven (vs. 2) and
the tongues of fire (vs. 3) both are reminiscent of Sinai (see
Exod 19:16, 18; Deut 5:4–5). Philo's comments show how the
Sinai theophany was understood in Hellenistic Judaism pri-
or to the time of Luke-Acts.

> God wrought on this occasion a miracle . . . by bidding an in-
> visible *sound* to be created in the air . . . which giving shape
> and tension to the air and changing it to *flaming fire*, sounded
> forth like the breath through a trumpet (*The Decalogue*, 9:33;
> see Philo's *Special Laws* 2:31:188–89).

In addition to the sound and the fire, Philo speaks of the
speech that could be understood by all of the audience.

> Then from the midst of the *fire* . . . there sounded forth to their
> utter amazement a *voice*, for the flame became *articulate speech
> in the language familiar to the audience* (*The Decalogue*, 11:46).

This is very much the same thing that one finds in the later
Jewish Midrash *Tanhuma* 26c:

> Although the ten commandments were promulgated with a
> single sound, it says, "All people heard the voices"; it follows
> then that when the voice went forth it was divided into seven
> voices and then went into seventy tongues, and every people
> received the law in their own language (*BC*, 5:116).

Sound, fire, and speech understood by all people were characteristic of the Sinai theophany. The same ingredients are
found in the Pentecostal events of the New Covenant.

In telling his story this way, the Evangelist seems to be
describing xenolalia, a variation of glossolalia found repeat-
edly in Christian history. It is similar to the cases of modern
people who claim to hear their own language being spoken
by persons with the gift of tongues. It may be that "tongues
of men and of angels" in 1 Cor 13:1 refers first to xenolalia
and then to glossolalia. In any case, a sharp distinction between what Luke describes here and what he describes elsewhere (e.g., 10:46; 19:6) cannot be drawn. They are two sides
of the same coin.

(2) After a description of the Pentecostal phenomena in
2:1–11, there is a long section (vss. 12–36) composed of two
speeches: the mockers' speech (vs. 13) and Peter's speech
(vss. 14–36). The mockers' speech gives the incorrect interpretation of the phenomena: "They are filled with new wine"
(vs. 13). Peter's speech gives what for the Evangelist is the
correct interpretation. The speech first says what the Pentecostal events do not mean (vss. 14–15): "these men are not
drunk as you suppose, since it is only nine A.M." Then the
speech says what the phenomena do mean (vss. 16–36). (a)
These happenings are the fulfillment of OT prophecy (vss.
14–21). Joel 2:28–32's prediction that God would one day
pour out his Spirit on all flesh has come to pass. (b) These
events are also the gift of the exalted Christ (vss. 22–36; Luke
3:16; see Eph 4:8–16). "He has poured out this which you see
and hear" (vs. 33).

(3) Acts 2:37–40 consists of a dialogue explaining the
proper response to the Pentecostal phenomena and their correct interpretation. There is first the hearers' query (vs. 37):
"Brethren, what shall we do?" Then there is Peter's response

(vss. 38–40): "Repent, and be baptized every one of you in the name of Jesus Christ." That is, do an about face in your life's orientation and attach yourself to Jesus (see Luke 23:26, a microcosm of the Lukan understanding of discipleship). The benefits of this include forgiveness of sins (see 10:43; 13:38) and reception of the Holy Spirit (vs. 38).

(a) It would be a mistake to take this passage as evidence that Luke-Acts links the reception of the Holy Spirit exclusively to baptism. There is no clear-cut theological or ecclesiastical pattern of how and when the Spirit can be expected to be given in Luke-Acts. In Acts 8:12–17 the Samaritan converts to Christianity were baptized without receiving the Spirit. Their experience of the Spirit came with the laying on of the apostles' hands. In 10:44–48, Cornelius and his family received the gift of the Spirit before they were baptized. In 19:5–6 the Spirit comes on the disciples of John the Baptist after their baptism in the name of Jesus and in connection with Paul's laying hands on them. If the Evangelist had any preference, it would seem to be reflected in the career of Jesus where after his baptism and while he was praying (Luke 3:21–22) the Spirit descended on him, foreshadowing the disciples' experience. No doubt the diversity evidenced in the narrative of Acts reflects the diversity of experience in the church of Luke's own day.

(b) It would likewise be a mistake to take this passage as proof that tongues were, for Luke, a necessary evidence of the baptism with the Holy Spirit. Although glossolalia or xenolalia is often a part of the experience of the Holy Spirit in Acts, it is not always so (e.g., 4:31 which in the pattern of Acts 1—5 is parallel to Acts 2; 8:17; 9:17–18, etc.).

(c) It would further be a mistake to think of Pentecost as a once-for-all event for the Evangelist. In Acts the outpouring of the Holy Spirit is depicted as repeatable in the life of the church (e.g., 4:31; 8:17; 10:1—11:18; 19:1–6).

(4) A narrative (vss. 41–47) telling of the results of the Pentecostal events and their proper interpretation concludes the section. The results are primarily two. (a) Evangelistic outreach results from the empowered witness of the apostles (vss. 41, 47b). (b) The establishment of a new kind of community results from the empowering and the outreach. It includes the nurture of the new converts (vss. 42, 46), corporate

worship (vss. 42, 46), and a unity that manifested itself in a sharing of possessions (vss. 44–45). The disciples are now empowered for the task of witness and proceed straightaway to carry out their commission (Acts 1:8). They do not neglect to nurture those evangelized, however. Futhermore, their common life gives evidence of the difference the Spirit makes. It is difficult to avoid hearing the author say that the Spirit has reversed Babel's curse (see Gen 11).

A sermon based on this text might be entitled "Empowering and Its Effects." The introduction would set the stage. In Acts 1:15–26 we see a petition and its answer side by side in the narrative. Acts 1:14 and chapter 2, though separated in the narrative flow by 1:15–26, also belong together as petition and answer. The risen Jesus had said to wait for the empowering (Luke 24:49; Acts 1:4–5, 8). The earthly Jesus had said to pray for the Holy Spirit (Luke 11:13). So while they wait, the disciples pray for the promise of the Father, the empowering of the Holy Spirit (Acts 1:14). In chapter 2 the Evangelist tells us what an answer to that prayer looks like. In Acts 2 we get a glimpse of empowering and its effects. Four things may be said about this empowering. First, it was a recognizable experience. In Luke-Acts the gift of the Holy Spirit is an experience of which the person is consciously aware and sometimes others as well. This is the significance of describing the phenomena that accompany the events. It would also be why in Acts 8 the Evangelist can say the Samaritans had been baptized but had not yet received the Spirit. In this Luke agrees with Paul (e.g., Rom 15:18–19; 1 Cor 2:3–5; Gal 3:1–5; 1 Thess 1:5, etc.). Second, the empowering was rooted in Scripture (Acts 2:17–21). Third, it was related to Jesus in a twofold way. On the one hand, he promised it (Luke 24:49; Acts 1:4–5, 8). On the other hand, he gave it (Luke 3:16; Acts 2:33). Fourth, the empowering was a repeatable experience (e.g., Acts 4:31; 8; 9; 10–11; 19). Two things may be said about the effects of the empowering. First, it resulted in outreach or evangelism (Acts 2:37–41, 47b). Second, it resulted in the creation of community (Acts 2:42, 44–46). In conclusion one should note that just as empowering follows petition, so evangelism and Christian unity or community follow Pentecost. The empowering, moreover, is repeatable. So pray!

The Shape of Christian Mission (3:1—4:31)

Acts 2:17–21 has Peter interpret the Pentecostal phenomena as a fulfillment of Joel 2:28–32. Part of this prophecy that is fulfilled reads: "And I will show . . . *signs* on the earth beneath" (Joel 2:19). In Acts 2:43 a summary statement tells us that "many . . . *signs* were done through the apostles." Acts 3:1–10 gives a concrete illustration of the signs done by the apostles. A man lame from birth is healed. What immediately follows is an attempt to interpret the sign by the apostles (3:16; 4:9–12) and to come to terms with it by the authorities (4:7, 14, 16, 22). The section concludes with the Christians' prayer to God which involves a petition for more *signs* (4:30).

The surface structure of the unit (3:1—4:31) reflects this focus on signs. The unit falls into three parts: (1) the miracle story (3:1–10) telling of the healing of the lame man; (2) the apostolic witness (3:11—4:23) which involves both an interpretation of the healing before the people (3:11–26) and its explanation before the rulers (4:1–23); and (3) a prayer scene (4:24–30) containing a petition (vss. 24–30) and its answer (vs. 31). Each part deserves some further attention.

(1) Acts 3:1–10 is a typical miracle story with its statement of the problem ("lame from birth"—vs. 2), its description of the cure ("in the name of Jesus of Nazareth, walk"—vs. 6), and its reference to the response to the sign ("they were filled with wonder and amazement"—vs. 10b). Its Lukan context, however, determines how it is to be understood. In the first place, it is a Lukan belief that a valid testimony to Christ requires two prominent witnesses, in accordance with Deut 19:15, namely, the witness of the apostles and the witness of the Holy Spirit. Acts 5:32 makes it explicit: "we are witnesses to these things, and so is the Holy Spirit whom God has given to those who obey him." The same viewpoint is found in Heb 2:3b–4: "it was attested to us by those who heard the Lord, while God also bore witness by signs and wonders and various miracles and by gifts of the Holy Spirit distributed according to his will." Paul echoes the same idea in 1 Thess 1:5, 1 Cor 2:3–5, and Rom 15:18–19. The signs are the Holy Spirit's witness to the resurrection of Jesus (Acts 2:33—"Being therefore exalted at the right hand of God, and having received from the Father the promise of the Holy

Spirit, he has poured out this which you see and hear."). The Holy Spirit not only empowers the apostles to give a bold witness but also, through them, bears a witness of his own. By the mouths of two witnesses is the authority of Jesus established. This healing of the lame man, then, is the Holy Spirit's testimony to the status of Jesus as Lord.

In the second place, in Luke-Acts salvation encompasses the whole person (e.g., Luke 4:18–19; 4:43 against the background of 4:31–37, 38–39, 40–41; 5:17–26; 7:18–23; 8:43–48; 13:10–17; 18:35–43; 19:1–10; Acts 10:36–38, etc.). The physical healings of the bodies of the afflicted are foretastes of the resurrection from the dead, just as one's conversion is a foretaste of the ultimate redemption from all evil. There is in Luke-Acts no reduction of salvation to a purely spiritual transaction any more than there is a reduction of it to a purely physical reality. The whole person is affected.

In the third place, the sign is not a magical event. It involves faith (3:16). Any prior faith in the story, however, is not that of the man healed; there is no evidence of that until after the event (3:8–9—"praising God" is a Lukan equivalent to a response of faith; see Luke 17:11–19, especially vss. 18–19; "glorifying God" is another equivalent, as in Luke 18:42–43). From Luke's point of view, to be healed is not the same as being saved (Luke 17:11–19) but healing may evoke faith and result in salvation, as obviously the Evangelist believed happened here (Acts 4:12). If there was faith prior to the healing, it was the apostles' faith. Vs. 16 seems to refer first to the prior faith of the apostles, then to the subsequent faith of the man evoked through Jesus' act on his behalf. If faith (human response to the divine initiative) is involved, then this sign cannot be designated as magic (human control of the divine powers to make them work for us). Luke-Acts wants to distance the Christian movement from magic (e.g., Acts 8:9–11, 19–24; 13:6–12; 19:18–19). The sign is the result of the Holy Spirit's witness, not of human attempts to control the numinous world.

(2) If Acts 3:1–10 gave the divine witness, 3:11—4:23 gives the apostolic witness to Jesus' authority. This witness involves an interpretation of the healing first before the people (3:11–26) and then before the rulers (4:1–23). On the one hand, 3:11–26, the witness before the people, is held together

by an inclusion: "the people" in 3:11 and 4:1a. The scene is set in 3:11: "All the people ran together to them ... astounded." Peter's speech in 3:12–26 involves two main components. There is first an explanation of how the healing happened (vss. 12–16). It was through the name of Jesus (vs. 16), not through the power or piety of the apostles (vs. 12— see Acts 14:14–18). There is then a call for repentance (vss. 17–26). The ignorance of the pre-Easter period may be over-looked (vs. 17) but, given the new evidence, repentance is the only acceptable response (vss. 19–23). It is not until all has been said that needs to be said that the officials interrupt the speech.

On the other hand, 4:1–23, gives the apostolic witness before the Council. The beginning of the section is signalled by "they arrested them" (4:3); the end by "they were re-leased" (4:23). Within these boundaries there are two scenes. Scene One (4:1b–12) contains three movements: (a) the arrest of the apostles (vss. 1b–3); (b) the Council gathers and in-quires (vss. 5–7); and (c) Peter's speech (vss. 8–12). The speech does two things. It explains how the healing hap-pened (vss. 8b–10): by the name of Jesus. It also proclaims salvation generally through Jesus (vss. 11–12): "no other name ... by which we must be saved." In speaking thusly, vs. 8 says Peter was "filled with the Holy Spirit." This speech fulfills the words of Jesus in Luke 12:11–12 (see Luke 21:12–15): "the Holy Spirit will teach you in that very hour what you ought to say." Scene Two (4:13–23) also contains three movements: (a) the Council deliberates and speaks (vss. 13–18)—"they charged them not to speak or teach at all in the name of Jesus" (vs. 18); (b) Peter and John answer (vss. 19–20)—"we cannot but speak of what we have seen and heard" (vs. 20b; see Socrates' statement to the court that condemned him; *Antigone*; and 2 Macc 7:2); and (c) the re-lease of the apostles (vss. 21–23).

(3) Acts 4:24–31 narrates a prayer scene consisting of the church's petition (vss. 24–30) in a form generally reminiscent of Isa 37:16–20 together with the petition's answer (vs. 31). The petition addresses God as "Sovereign Lord" and begins with two examples of God's control (he is Creator—vs. 24; his plan for history is being realized as evidenced by the fulfill-ment of prophecy—vss. 25–28). It then asks for two things:

that they might speak the word with all boldness (vs. 29), and that God would accompany their testimony with his own, in signs (vs. 30). The first part of the petition is answered immediately: "And when they had prayed, the place in which they were gathered together was shaken (a typical accompaniment of a theophany—e.g., Exod 19:18; Isa 6:4; Vergil, *Aeneid*, 3:88–91); and they were all filled with the Holy Spirit and spoke the word of God with boldness" (vs. 31). The second part would be answered in 5:12, 15–16. The motif of the twofold witness continues to the very end of this unit.

In this unit the witness to Jesus is understood to consist both of deeds (signs) and words. The word without the deed is insufficient because there is little interest in the abstractions of another's system of belief. It takes the deeds to peak the interest and raise the questions. Likewise, the deed without the word is incomplete. Only if the true meaning of the event is known can one discern the proper response to make to it. In Luke-Acts, the deed and the word are held together as the necessary dual testimony to the truth about Jesus.

A sermon based on this text might be called "The Shape of Christian Mission." The introduction poses the question raised by the Lukan narrative. Having been empowered by the Holy Spirit, the apostles are now engaged in mission in fulfillment of the risen Jesus' word (Acts 1:8). The question is: what shape does the Christian mission take? Acts 3:1—4:31 gives us a picture of what it looks like. According to this text, there is a rhythm of dispersal and assembly, of witness and worship. On the one hand, the church dispersed bears witness. This is done by the Christians as they go about their normal routine (3:1–10). The point is the same as that made in Matt 28:19–20 where the participle should be translated, "As you go, make disciples." This witness is made in deed and in word (3:1—4:12). It is made in deed to the whole person (3:1–10) and is accompanied by an explanation (3:11—4:12). On the other hand, the church assembled shares and worships (see Heb 10:25; Ignatius, *To Ephesians*, 13:1–2). Their fellowship is mentioned in Acts 4:23–24 (see 2:44–46). Their worship is accented in 4:24–31. It involves both prayer (4:24–30; see Luke 3:21–22 followed by 4:16—5:15; then 5:16; see 6:12, etc.) and further empowering (4:31). A conclusion to such a sermon would need to pull together the Lukan vision.

An empowered church lives in a rhythm of witness and worship—a witness to the whole person, a worship that empowers and gives boldness for further witness.

Putting Possessions in Their Place (4:32—5:11)

Acts 4:31 told of the answer to the community's prayer. "They spoke the word of God with boldness." The summary that follows (vss. 32–35) falls into an ABA' pattern.

> A—The fellowship of the Christian community (vs. 32)
> B—The powerful witness of the apostles (vs. 33)
> A'—The fellowship of the Christian community (vss. 34–35)

The B component picks up the theme of 4:31b and reaffirms it. The community empowered by the Spirit engages in a bold and powerful witness/mission. The A and A' components advance the discussion by focusing on the inner life of the church (5:11). This thought unit's concern is primarily with the fellowship (inner life) of the Christian community.

The surface structure falls into two parts. (1) There is the opening summary with its ABA' pattern which indicates the concern for Christian fellowship (4:32–35). (2) There are then two examples or illustrations of the communal life of the empowered disciples. One is a positive example (4:36–37); the other is a negative one (5:1–11). The positive example says what Christian fellowship is like; the negative one what it is not like.

(1) Acts 4:32–35 describes the fellowship of the Christian community empowered by the Holy Spirit as the realization of both pagan and Jewish ideals. On the one hand, vs. 32's, "no one said that any of the things which he possessed was his own, but they had everything in common," echoes Greco-Roman ideals about friendship. Aristotle said: "Among friends everything is common is quite correct, for friendship consists in sharing" (*Ethics* 8:11; 1159B, 31). Euripides quoted the saying. For example, "True friends cling not to private property; their wealth is shared in close community" (*Andromache* 376–77). Plutarch said: "Friends possess everything in common" (*Dialogue on Love* 21:9; 967E). On the other hand, vs. 34's, "there was not a needy person among them," echoes both Jewish and Greco-Roman ideals. In Deut 15:4, as part of an

idealized picture of the future of Israel in Canaan, we hear: "But there will be no poor among you." Likewise, in Seneca's *Epistle* 90:38 we hear this Stoic speak of the primitive period of ideal time when "you could not find a single pauper." The Evangelist is saying that the primitive church realizes the ideals of friendship, fellowship, and common concern held by pagan and Jew alike. In so doing Luke was verbalizing values held generally by the early Christians near his time. The *Epistle of Barnabas* 19:8 says: "You shall share everything with your neighbor, and shall not call things your own." The *Didache* 4:8 puts it this way: "You shall not turn the needy away, but you shall share everything with your brother, and you shall not say it is your own."

The sharing of material possessions with one another was the outward manifestation of a deeper spiritual unity. Vs. 32a says: "Now the company of those who believed were of one heart and soul." This also reflects Greco-Roman beliefs. Diogenes Laertius (*Lives of Eminent Philosophers* 5:20) quotes Aristotle as saying that a friend is one soul dwelling in two bodies. Cicero said that the essence of friendship lies in the formation of a single soul from several (*On Friendship* 25:92). Plutarch taught that friends "though existing in separate bodies, actively unite and fuse their souls together, no longer wishing or considering themselves to be two separate beings" (*Dialogue on Love* 21:9; 967E). The Evangelist again depicts the primitive church as having realized this ideal. Other Christians of Luke's time also recognized that the sharing of possessions grew out of a sharing at a deeper level. The *Didache* 4:8 says: "For if you share in what is immortal, how much more in mortal things." Barnabas 19:8 reads: "For if you share what is imperishable, how much more the things that are perishable." In these two writings using the Two Ways formula, the argument is "how much more." In Luke-Acts the argument is that the Christians have realized the Greco-Roman ideals of friendship. The reason for this fulfillment of cultural ideals was the empowering of the Spirit (4:31; chap. 2).

It is interesting to note that here the apostles are responsible both for the preaching (vs. 34) and for the administration of funds (vs. 35). This was soon to be changed (6:1–6). The results of the Spirit's empowering were both evangelism and the creation of deep fellowship. It would soon be necessary to recognize that the same persons could not implement both. A division of labor would soon be called for.

(2) Acts 4:36—5:11 narrates both a concrete example of this Christian fellowship (4:36–37) and a perversion of it (5:1–11). (a) Barnabas (vss. 36–37) sold a field and brought the money and laid it at the apostles' feet (see vs. 35a where "and laid it at the apostles' feet" concludes the summary). In Lukan thought, the Holy Spirit indwells the community ("they were filled with the Holy Spirit"—vs. 31). The Spirit's inner leading is not only to mission (1.8; 4:31b) but also to community (4:32a; 2:44–45). This community fellowship is first of all spiritual ("of one heart and soul"—vs. 32a). This spiritual unity, however, spills over into the physical, financial world of believers (vs. 32b; 34–35). This is part of the Lukan belief that wealth is properly used when it builds relationships and community (Luke 12:33–34; 16:9; Acts 2:44–45; 11:27–30; 24:17). What concerns our Evangelist are the social benefits of wealth rightly used. What he wants to avoid is the use of wealth in the service of private indulgence. Moreover, wealth is properly used if the disciples live out of their being filled with the Holy Spirit. Only if they do not follow the Spirit's leading will they use wealth for private indulgence instead of to express and to build community. Barnabas is depicted here as one who follows the Spirit's leading (see 11:24).

(b) Ananias and Sapphira illustrate the desire to use their wealth for their personal indulgence while at the same time appearing to embody the ideals of true friendship. While they pretend to participate in the Christian fellowship, they manifest a secret independence from the community. Like Achan in Josh 7 and Judas in Luke-Acts (Luke 22:3ff.), the "love of money" is what separates them from the deep fellowship of the disciples. The love of money in the case both of Judas and of Ananias and Sapphira is linked with Satan (Luke 22:3—"Satan entered Judas"; Acts 5:3—"Satan filled your heart"). Luke believes that, through the temptation of money, Satan can get control of a personality (see Luke 8:14). Although Ananias and Sapphira pretended to be following the Spirit's leading, they were of a divided heart. This would seem, in part, to be what Luke 12:10 means by blaspheming the Holy Spirit. Although the immediate context of Luke 12:10 is speaking about witness, the implication about Christian unity is implicit, given the context of Luke-Acts as a whole. Either the suppression of the Spirit's leading to witness in a threatening situation or the perversion of his urging to deep fellowship because of a love of money are an attempt to lie to the Holy Spirit (to say, "I am following your leading," when in reality I am not). Their split between public profession and inner reality is discerned by Peter. The power of God described in Heb 4:13 is here given to the apostle. This spiritual discernment (1 Cor 12:10—"the ability to discern spirits") belongs to the Spirit-empowered disciples just as it did to the Spirit-empowered Jesus (e.g., Luke 7:36–50). Just as in 1 Cor 11:29–30, failure to discern the body (i.e., act in the interests of Christian unity) results in divine judgment. Like Judas (Acts 1:18–19), Ananias and Sapphira do not live to enjoy their gain (Acts 5:5, 10; see Luke 12:15–21).

A sermon based on this passage might be entitled "Putting Possessions in Their Place." The introduction would need to set the stage. Empowering by the Holy Spirit produces unity (4:32, 34–35; 2:44–45) as well as evangelistic outreach (4:33, 31b). One area this spiritual unity affects is that of possessions. Since possessions are extensions of our selfhood, when we are bonded to others by the Holy Spirit, it changes our use of possessions and their place in our lives. The text speaks both about the wrong place and the right place of possessions in Christians' lives. On the one side, Acts 5:1–11 focuses on the wrong place. When possessions are used to express our separation from others and to separate further, they occupy the wrong place. This selfishness indicates a divided mind. The basis of such a divided mind is twofold: (1) the love of money (2) which gives Satan an opening to our hearts. On the other side, 4:32–37 speaks about the right place for possessions in Christian existence. When possessions are used generously with resulting social benefits, they occupy a right place. The basis of this generosity is twofold: (1) the deep unity with other believers (4:32a) (2) which results from being filled with the Spirit and following his leading. A fitting conclusion would sum up the Lukan point. A Spirit-filled community (4:31) is one in which there is a deep spiritual unity (4:32a) that expresses itself in a lifestyle that puts possessions in their place.

Dealing with Religious Innovation (5:12–42)

In Acts 4:29–30, the church assembled had prayed for two things: (1) that they might speak the word with boldness (vs. 29); and (2) that God would go on bearing witness through healings, signs, and wonders (vs. 30). The prayer is answered in stages. The answer to the first petition comes in 4:31 ("spoke the word of God with boldness") and in 4:33 ("gave their testimony"). The answer to the second comes in 5:12a, 15–16 ("many signs and wonders were done"; "the sick and those afflicted with unclean spirits ... were healed"). This dual witness of apostles and the Holy Spirit effected numerous conversions (vs. 14). These healings produced the same result within the religious establishment that the healing of the lame man in 3:1–10 had produced earlier (4:1–22): backlash! Acts 5:17–42 gives us a picture of an ecclesiastical establishment's attempts to deal with religious innovation within its ranks (see Luke 19:47—21:4).

The surface structure falls into five scenes, each of which consists first of the establishment's initiative against the Christians to halt their innovations and then of the various responses to those initiatives (5:17–21a; 21b–27a; 27b–32; 33–39; 40–42). (1) In the first scene (17–21a), the Sadducees, filled with jealousy, arrest the apostles and put them in the common prison (vss. 17–18; see 4:3; 12:3; 16:23; Luke 21:12). The divine response to the Saducean initiative takes the form of an angel's (in whose existence the Sadducees did not believe—23:8) opening the doors, bringing them out, and commissioning them to speak to the people (vss. 19–20; see 12:7–11; 16:25–34). The effect of this scene on the hearer of the narrative is to affirm that the Christian movement is of God.

(2) In the second scene (vss. 21b–27a), the Council gathers and sends for the prisoners (vs. 21c). The narrative that follows says first that the apostles were not found in prison (vss. 22–24); "the prison (was) securely locked and the sentries (were) standing at the doors, but when we opened it we found no one inside." It then says that the apostles were

found in the Temple (vs. 25), obeying the angelic command of vs. 20 (remember 1:8). Thereupon the captain and his officers bring them, but without violence (vss. 26–27a). The effect of scene two on the hearer is to create the impression that the establishment is up against a mightier opponent.

(3) In scene three (vss. 27b–32), the council questions the apostles about their disobedience to an earlier command not to teach in Jesus' name (vss. 27b–28; see 4:17–18). The apostolic response is a bold one: "we must obey God rather than men" (vs. 29). This type of response is typical of the Lukan heroes (see 4:19–20; 26:19). It would have also been considered the thing to do in the Mediterranean world of the time. For example, in Plutarch's biography of Caius Marcius Coriolanus we hear of one Titus Latinus, quiet and modest, free from superstitious fears and vain pretensions, who had a vision of Jupiter bidding him to tell the Senate a certain message. Titus neglected to do as bidden, even after having the vision a second and third time. Whereupon he suffered the loss of an excellent son by death and himself became suddenly palsied. He was then brought to the Senate on a litter. No sooner had he delivered the message than at once he felt the strength return to his body. He rose up and walked away without aid, much to the amazement of all. In antiquity it was believed necessary to obey heavenly commissions. The apostles' behavior here is depicted as exemplary. They obey the heavenly vision without hesitation. The effect of this scene on the hearer is once again to identify the Christian movement with the divine will.

(4) In scene four (vss. 33–39), the Council wants to kill the apostles (vs. 33). This initiative is aborted by the intervention of one of their own number, Gamaliel the Pharisee (vss. 34–39). The speech is preceded by a statement of Gamaliel's virtues: "a teacher of the law, held in honor by all the people (vs. 34). The speech consists of two historical examples of religious innovations that came to nought (Theudas and Judas the Galilean), followed by its conclusion. "So in the present case . . ., keep away from those men and let them alone; for if this plan . . . is of men, it will fail; but if it is of God, you will not be able to overthrow them. You might even be found opposing God" (vss. 38–39). The effect of this speech on the

hearer who already knows that the apostles represent God is to throw all of the weight on "let them alone. Do not oppose God." To wait and see is the better wisdom.

(5) In scene five (vss. 40–42), the Council takes Gamaliel's advice and does not kill the apostles. The body does, however, beat them and charge them again not to speak in the name of Jesus (vs. 40). The command is as ineffective as the earlier one (4:17–18). "And every day . . . they did not cease teaching and preaching Jesus as the Christ" (vs. 42). Moreover, they rejoiced that they were counted worthy to suffer dishonor for the name (vs. 41; Luke 6:22–23; see Phil 1:29). The apostles are here shown to be continuing to obey God in spite of threats and pain. The total effect of this section on the hearer is that the established order is being overwhelmed by the new currents in the unfolding of God's plan.

A sermon based on this passage might be entitled "Dealing with Religious Innovation." The introduction should set the stage. When the Holy Spirit is poured out on God's people, there are new developments and emphases that result. These religious innovations raise questions both for the innovators and for the traditional community. How should each act in these circumstances? Two things may be said about the innovators. First, they are objects of divine protection (5:17–26). Second, they are subjects under divine orders (5:27–32, 40–42) who must take a stand (5:29—"we must obey God rather than man") and who must bear the consequences (5:40–41—"suffer dishonor for the name"). The text also says two things about the traditional community. On the one hand, the text tells the traditional community what not to do: do not use force against innovators (5:33). On the other hand, it also says what the traditional community should do in the face of innovation: wait and see (5:34–39). Verses 38b–39 sum it up well: "if this . . . is of men, it will fail; but if it is of God, you will not be able to overthrow them. You might even be found opposing God." The conclusion would sum up the matter. In times of religious innovation, the innovators will have to obey God and bear the consequences, trusting themselves to divine protection. The traditional community will have to refrain from force, wait and see. Both stances are based on the confidence that what is of God will ultimately be vindicated, while what is not of God will fail.

Making Structural Forms for Spiritual Reality (6:1-7)

Acts 6:1-7 is a thought unit held together by an inclusion: "the disciples were increasing" (*plethunonton*—vs. 1) and "the number of the disciples multiplied" (*eplethuneto*—vs. 7). The core of the unit, vss. 1-6, reflects an OT form used for "the choice of supplementary leadership" (e.g., Exod 18: 14-25; Num 27:12-23). This Gattung consisted of four components: (1) the problem (Exod 18:14-18; Num 27:12-14); (2) the proposed solution (Exod 18:19-23; Num 27:15-17); (3) the qualifications of the new leadership (Exod 18:21; Num 27:18-21); and (4) the setting apart of the new leaders (Exod 18:25; Num 27:22-23). In line with his usual imitation of the LXX, the Lukan Evangelist shapes both Acts 1:15-26 and 6:1-6 in accord with this form: (1) the problem (Acts 1:15-20; 6:1-2); (2) the proposed solution (Acts 1:21a; 6:3a, 4); (3) the qualifications of the new leadership (Acts 1:21b-22; 6:3b) and (4) the setting apart of the new leaders (Act 1:23-26; 6:5-6). The very choice of this Gattung shows the passage's thrust to be on the selection of new and additional leadership for the community of disciples.

Each component of the Gattung in 6:1-6 needs further examination. (1) Acts 2:45 ("and they sold their possessions and goods and distributed them *all*, as any had need") and 4:34-35 ("There was not a needy person among them . . . distribution was made to each as *any* had need") speak of the overflow of the spiritual unity of the earliest disciples. The needs of any and all were met. Success took its toll, however. "When the disciples were increasing in number, the Hellenists (Greek-speaking Jewish Christians—see 6:9) murmured against the Hebrews (Aramaic speaking Jewish Christians) because their widows were neglected in the daily distribution" (vs. 1). Apparently the Christians had already set up some structure for caring for the needy analogous to the Jewish practice but it was not working well. This is half of the problem: a diverse membership that presents structural problems. The other half of the problem comes in vs. 2:

"The twelve ... said: 'It is not right that we should give up preaching the word of God to serve tables.' '" There was a practical need to have the structures of the community reflect the spiritual oneness of the disciples. There was also the problem that the Twelve's self concept or calling did not match up with the need. Here we have the two sides of the problem.

(2) The solution that is proposed is for additional leadership in the community: "brethren, pick out from among you seven men ... whom we may appoint to this duty. But we will devote ourselves to prayer and to the ministry of the word" (vss. 3a, 4). In other words, what is proposed is a division of labor within the leadership. This was something that would have been part of Luke's readers' way of thinking, not only because of past Christian practice (1 Cor 12:4–7, 28–30; see "apostles ... administrators") but also because of Moses' example (Exod 18:19–20, 23).

(3) The qualifications of the new leadership are both stated explicitly (vs. 3b) and hinted at (vs. 5; see vs. 9). It is explicitly directed that they should be "of good repute, full of the Spirit and of wisdom" (see 1 Tim 3:8–13). Those entrusted with setting up and implementing the structures of the community's life, just as the apostles, were to be "full of the Spirit." This was exactly the kind of people they did, in fact, choose: "they chose Stephen, a man full of faith and of the Holy Spirit" (vs. 5). Only thereby could the structures reflect the spiritual basis of the community's life. The choice of these seven indicates an implicit criterion as well. At least some of them, maybe all judging from their Greek names, came from the segment of the church that felt discriminated against. Not only did they need to have a good reputation, be wise and spiritual, they also needed to represent the interests of the oppressed.

(4) The choice of the Seven was apparently made by the congregation (vss. 3, 6) and confirmed by the apostles in terms of the Lord's leading (vs. 6). This indicates the broad-based decision making of the early Christians. It also reflects the theological perspective of the Evangelist in yet another way. That all make the choice reflects the Lukan belief that all have the Spirit living in and guiding them. That the twelve confirm the community's decision is in line with the

Lukan theme that they are the bearers and guardians of the true tradition. In other words, experience and tradition interact to yield a proper result.

Taken together, these four components make up the biblical Gattung for the choice of supplementary leadership. The problem of unintentional structural injustice is remedied by the recognition of a diversity of gifts and functions within the church's leadership and by the recognition that every segment of the community's membership needs to be represented in that leadership.

Acts 6:7 is a summary statement added to the Gattung of vss. 1–6. It's presence indicates that once again (cf. 2:47b; 4:33; 5:14) the unity of the community yields evangelistic benefits. Even "a great many of the priests," who were formerly hostile (4:1), "were obedient to the faith."

This text may yield a sermon entitled, "Making Structural Forms for Spiritual Reality." This passage, like Phil 2:12–13 ("work out your—plural—own salvation"), speaks of the community's working out in their corporate life the inner spiritual realities they have experienced. Here a new problem, resulting from numerical success and a diversified membership, calls for a new organizational structure to embody the spiritual realities of the community. There are diversities of function and work in the church (1 Cor 12:4–6). There is a ministry of the word (outreach) and there is a serving of tables (administration). Although formerly handled by one group, the apostles (4:35), this was no longer possible. This text in Acts makes three points.

First, outreach, successfully done, demands consolidation. Success, understood both as increased numbers and diversified membership, creates structural problems. Acts 2:45 and 4:34–35 indicate that the problem was not bad intention. The problem lay in the implementation (compare 4:35 with 6:2) of good intentions.

Second, consolidation, to be properly done, requires three things. (1) It requires structures that guarantee that the spiritual unity is expressed in the organized community behavior and that do not cause neglect of the ministry of outreach. (2) It requires staff, both people with good reputation, wisdom, and spirituality, and people who represent the interests of all the membership. (3) It requires a selection process reflecting both the congregational will as it expresses the common experience of the Spirit and the mind of the guardians of the tradition of the earthly Jesus.

Third, consolidation, properly done, fosters further outreach. "Just structures" in the life of the church are crucial to further evangelization.

In conclusion, we may note the words of Justin Martyr (*I Apology* 14:2–3), written not far from the time of Luke-Acts: "We who once coveted most greedily the wealth and fortunes of others, now place in common the goods we possess, dividing them with all the needy." This Christian practice was possible only when the spiritual unity of the believers was matched by structures that reflected this unity and was administered in such a way as to guarantee the inner intention of the community. Acts 6:1–7 tells of an attempt to implement a structural guarantee that the spiritual unity of the believers be realized in practice.

When Dialogue Fails (6:8—8:4)

Acts 6:8—8:4 is a unit beginning (6:8) and ending (8:4) on the note of witness. The section falls into an ABA' pattern.

> A—narrative about events leading up to Stephen's speech (6:8–15)
> B—Question and answer sequence (7:1–53)
> A'—narrative about the effects of Stephen's speech (7:54—8:4).

Each of these components needs investigation.

(1) Acts 6:8–15 (A in the pattern) tells of the events leading up to Stephen's speech. This subsection is held together by an inclusion (evidence of Stephen's spirituality in vss. 8 and 15). Its components are four. (a) Stephen's performance of wonders and signs (vs. 8) is a partial answer to the petition of 4:30 (see 4:12). The Holy Spirit is bearing witness to Jesus' resurrection (5:32). (b) This witness evokes disputes with Hellenistic Jews (see 21:27 where the opponents of Paul are also Hellenistic Jews). Stephen is triumphant in the disputations (vs. 10) like Jesus before him (Luke 19:47—21:4) and as the earthly Jesus had promised his disciples would be (Luke 21:15). (c) The defeated opposition then secures enough false charges against him to have him seized and brought before

the Council (vss. 11–12). (d) Before the Council Stephen's opponents set up false witnesses to charge him with antagonism to the Temple and to the law (vss. 13–14): "for we have heard him say that this Jesus of Nazareth will destroy this place, and will change the customs which Moses delivered to us." These are the same changes that will be made later against Paul (Acts 21:20–21, 28; 24:7; 25:8).

(2) Acts 7:1–53 (B in the pattern) is a question and answer sequence. In vs. 1 the high priest asks Stephen: "Is this so?" Vss. 2–53 are Stephen's answer to the two charges. The speech says in essence that his accusers, like their Jewish ancestors, are those who do not recognize the authority of Moses or keep his law. Their devotion to the Temple, moreover, is part of their disobedience. On the one hand, the speech points out that Israel for a long time has been going astray. (a) The Jewish fathers rejected Moses' authority in Egypt (vss. 27, 35). Nevertheless, it was the rejected one whom God made ruler and judge for them (vs. 35—listen to the echoes of Jesus' situation). (b) They also rejected Moses' authority in the wilderness (vss. 39–41): "our fathers refused to obey him, but thrust him aside, and in their hearts they turned to Egypt" (vs. 39), made the golden calf, and sacrificed to this idol (vss. 40–41). In this idolatry they violated the commandment against graven images (Exod 20:4). (c) Furthermore, in the land they departed from Moses' directions (vs. 44) when a temple was built (vss. 47–50) to replace the tent of witness made according to God's directions (see Heb 8—9 where the tabernacle is regarded as the true type of worship). This rejection of Moses' authority, moreover, was typical of the fathers' treatment of God's messengers generally. "Which of the prophets did not your fathers persecute? And they killed those who announced beforehand the coming of the Righteous One" (vs. 52a; see Luke 13:34; 6:22–23).

On the other hand, the speech says that the present conduct of the Jews is of a piece with that of the Jewish ancestors. (a) In betraying and murdering the Righteous One (vs. 52b), they have not listened to Moses who prophesied: "God will raise up for you a prophet from your brethren as he raised me up" (vs. 37; see 3:22–23; Deut 18:15–18; John 5:46–47). (b) In bearing false witness against Stephen (6:13–14), they violate the commandment in Exod 20:16.

When they kill Stephen in the verses following, they will violate yet another commandment (Exod 20:13). They are correctly described as those "who received the law . . . and did not keep it" (vs. 53). In conclusion, one would have to say that Stephen's response to the two charges is that his accusers and their ancestors, not he, are those who act against the authority of Moses and have changed what he delivered to us. The accusers stand accused!

(3) Acts 7:54—8:4 (A' in the pattern) tells about the effects of Stephen's speech. (a) As a result of Stephen's accusations, action was taken against him. His opponents were furious ("they ground their teeth against him"—vs. 54). When he verbalized his vision of the Son of Man standing at the right hand of God (vs. 56—i.e., Jesus in this place of authority indicates the correctness of the Christians' claims), Stephen's opponents cast him out of the city and stone him (vs. 58). The words of Jesus in Luke 21:16 are fulfilled: "and some of you they will put to death." His martyrdom is described in terms that echo the death of Jesus in Luke (Acts 7:59//Luke 23:46; Acts 7:60//Luke 23:34). The reader knows that his prayer for Jesus to receive his spirit is answered because of what the earthly Jesus taught (Luke 21:19—"By your endurance you will gain your lives."). The martyr has his reward (see *Martyrdom of Apollonius*—The Christian, Apollonius, says: "Proconsul Perenius, I thank my God for this sentence of yours which will bring me salvation.").

(b) Not only does Stephen's speech lead to his own death, it and his martyrdom result in a persecution of the larger church (8:1b—"On that day a great persecution arose against the church in Jerusalem; and they were all scattered throughout the region of Judea and Samaria, except the apostles."). Saul was especially fierce in his activities against the Christians (vs. 3). If the individual martyr had gained his reward by being received into the arms of the exalted Jesus, the Christian cause reaps its corporate benefits from the persecution also. "Now those who were scattered went about preaching the word" (vs. 4). In trying to beat out the flames of Christianity, its opponents had scattered sparks far and wide and only increased the scope of the fire (see Luke 23:43). As Justin Martyr put it: "the more we are persecuted, the more do others in ever increasing numbers embrace the faith and become worshipers of God through the name of Jesus" (*Dialogue* 110). The Stephen episode is, in Luke-Acts, the bridge over which the gospel marches unhindered out of Jerusalem.

This passage can be preached in a number of different ways. The sermon that stays closest to the text might be entitled, "When Dialogue Fails." The introduction would set the stage. When the Holy Spirit is poured out, even within the people of God there is resistance (6:8–10), sometimes even to the point of dishonesty (6:11–15). When dialogue fails and persecution proceeds, then, as before, it is a time for testimony (Luke 21:13). When persecuted, what do Christians do and for what do they hope? The Lukan answer is twofold.

First, in persecution Christians bear witness (see Luke 21:12–19). This witness is given both in word (7:2–53) and in deed (7:54–60). Second, in persecution Christians expect certain benefits. These benefits are both for themselves individually (Acts 7:59; see Luke 12:4–9; 21:16, 19) and for the cause of Christ generally (Acts 8:1, 4–8; 11:19–26). Even in suffering persecution, Christians fulfill the commission of their Lord (Acts 1:8). A conclusion could sum up. Although resistance to the Spirit-empowered testimony to Jesus may bring suffering, and even death, to the individual, persecution offers a time for testimony in word and deed. Even if the individual appears to lose to his/her persecutors, there is eternal gain for him/her and the spread of the gospel in the world. When dialogue fails and persecution follows, bear witness and expect the benefits to follow.

Another sermon might be "How to Honor the Book." This passage gives us a picture of some religious zealots who love the Temple (church) and the law (Bible) so much that they are determined to defend them against change, even if it means disobeying the Book. Their devotion to the Bible is a substitute for their obedience to God. In such a situation, Acts 6:8—8:4 says if you want to honor the Book, (1) do not defend it, rather (2) obey it.

Inclusive but Uncompromised (8:5–40)

Acts 8:4 said that the persecution of the church after the Stephen incident caused many Christians to be scattered abroad and that they preached as they went. Acts 8:5–40 nar-

rates two incidents of such preaching by Philip, one of the
Seven (6:5). The first, 8:5–25, focuses on Samaria; the second,
8:26–40, on the Ethiopian eunuch. Taken together the stories
tell of the disciples' fulfillment of the risen Jesus' commission in Acts 1:8: "you will be my witnesses in . . . Samaria
and to the end of the world."

The Samaria episode (8:5–25) consists of two acts. In the
first (vss. 5–13), Philip is center stage; in the second (vss.
14–25) Peter is central. The first act demonstrates that the
power of the Holy Spirit is greater than that of magic. This is
done in two stages. It is done initially by depicting the similarities between Philip's activity and that of Simon (vss. 5–8,
6–11). Both perform remarkable deeds (vss. 6, 11). As a result,
the Samaritans "gave heed" (*proseichon*, vss. 6, 11) to both.
The similarities are followed, however, by remarkable differences. The Samaritans generally believe Philip and are baptized, both men and women (vs. 12; see John 4:7–30). Those
who had witnessed the deeds of both recognized that Philip's
were the greater. Even the one who had practiced magic, Simon himself, believed and was baptized (vs. 13). What better
testimony can there be to the superiority of the Holy Spirit's
witness to Jesus over magic?

Vss. 14–25 compose the second act, a unit held together by
an inclusion ("they sent"—vs. 14; "they returned"—vs. 25).
This second act of the Samaritan drama falls into two parts.
On the one hand, the Samaritans receive the Holy Spirit well
after their bapitism through the laying on of the hands of
Peter and John (vss. 15–17;. These verses show the impossi-
bility of relegating the gift of the Holy Spirit to a set formula
(e.g., the Spirit is given at baptism). God is free! They also
presume that it can be known whether or not a person has
received the Spirit. The experience of the Holy Spirit for
Luke is an event that is both consciously known to the individual receiving and observable by others (see 10:45–46).
These verses also indicate that the inclusion of the Samaritans resulting from the persecution in Jerusalem and in fulfillment of the risen Jesus' commission was both recognized
by the Jerusalem apostles (who represent the true tradition)
and ratified by God (through the gift of the Spirit). In others
words, this outreach is legitimate.

On the other hand, Simon, who presumably had also received the Holy Spirit, asks to buy the power to impart the Spirit through the laying on of hands. He interprets the Christian experience of the Holy Spirit in magical terms. In magic one does what is necessary to gain control of spiritual powers in order to have them do one's bidding. Such knowledge and techniques were expensive (Acts 19:19). Acts is generally hostile to magic (e.g., 13:4–12; 19:19; see Luke 4:1–13). This passage is no exception. Simon's non-Christian interpretation of the reception and impartation of the Spirit is rebuked ("your silver perish with you"—vs. 20a); he is excommunicated ("you have neither part nor lot in this matter"—vs. 21a) and is called on to repent and to ask for forgiveness (vs. 22). Even this serious sin could be forgiven, but repentance was necessary. The story shows both the inclusiveness of the gospel (Samaritans, men and women, magicians) and the necessity for radical change in those so included. It also shows that the Holy Spirit is a gift from God (vs. 20) that comes neither as a result of the payment of a proper purchase price nor, apparently, as a result of moral perfection.

The episode of Philip's encounter with the Ethiopian eunuch (8:26–40) begins with two panels that are nicely balanced (vss. 26–28; 29–30). In the first (vss. 26–28) we hear: (a) an angel of the Lord said to Philip, "Go" (vs. 26); (b) and he went (vs. 27a); and (c) what he saw (vss. 27b–28): the Ethiopian eunuch (a Jew? a God-fearer?) in his chariot reading. In the second panel (vss. 29–30) we hear: (a) the Spirit said to Philip, "Go" (vs. 29); (b) so he ran to him (vs. 30a); and (c) what he heard (vs. 30b): the eunuch was reading from Isaiah the prophet. With this the foundation is laid for a dialogue between Philip and the eunuch which follows (vss. 30b–37). (a) Phillip said: "Do you understand what you are reading?" (b) The eunuch said: "How can I, unless someone guides me?" (c) The eunuch said: "About whom . . . does the propet say this? (d) Then Philip "told him the good news of Jesus." (e) The eunuch said: "What is to prevent my being baptized?" The outcome is twofold. First, the eunuch is baptized (vs. 38); then Philip is caught up by the Spirit (vss. 39–40).

This episode, like the previous one, points to the inclusiveness of the gospel. Normally eunuchs were considered outcasts of Israel (Deut 23:1). Isa 56:1–8, however, looked forward to a time when even eunuchs would be included in God's people. Acts 8:26–40 says that time has arrived. This fits the general Lukan theme that Jesus and the gospel include all sorts of undesirables (e.g., Luke 4:27–32; 7:36–50; 15:1–2). It also says that this inclusiveness is God's doing (vss. 26, 29, 39).

The thrust of this chapter is that all sorts of people are included in God's people: Samaritans, eunuchs, women as well as men, magicians as well as those impressed by magic. All can believe in Jesus, all can be baptized, all can receive the gift of the Holy Spirit, all can be fully included in the church. Such inclusion, however, calls for radical repentance. A Christian is not a magician who has gotten control of God through Jesus' name to make him do his/her bidding. Christians rather are those over whom God has gotten control so we will do his bidding. The chapter says: be included but be changed!

This chapter yields a sermon entitled, "Inclusive but Uncompromised." The introduction would note that the picture the Third Evangelist paints of the primitive church in Acts presents us with a community that is inclusive without being compromised (i.e., by worldly values). This is an achievement of monumental proportions. How can it be? The text answers our question in two stages.

In the first place, Acts 8 shows the church to be inclusive in its outreach. It is inclusive of racially and religiously mixed people (Samaritans), physically deformed people (eunuch), women as well as men, charlatans, dabblers in the occult (Simon), and those fascinated by the occult (the Samaritans). Its inclusiveness is due to the fact that the church is God-controlled, both by experience (the angel, the Spirit) and by tradition (both pre- and post-Easter tradition).

In the second place, Acts 8:5–40 shows the church demanding conversion of those included. This conversion is from a magical understanding of religion which tries to control God for one's own benefit to an understanding of religion in terms of grace, that is, to live out of a response to God's gift. The ground of this conversion rests on who God is and who we are. God is the one who, in biblical faith, always has the initiative. Humans wait for God, pray to God (Luke 18:1–8; Acts

1), respond to God, but never seize the initiative from God. From the Lukan vantage point the primitive community was able to be inclusive without being compromised because it let God have the initiative. On God's initiative, it was inclusive. It demanded of those included a conversion that allowed God to continue to have the initiative. Such a summation captures the essence of the Lukan message and of our contemporary need.

Discipleship—Two Types (9:1–31)

The story of Paul's conversion (call) is sandwiched in between the episodes of the Ethiopian eunuch (8:26–40) and the conversion of Cornelius (10:1—11:18). These two episodes establish the principle of a move to the ends of the earth (Acts 1:8). The narrative about Paul which lies between them depicts the divine choice of the one who will later (chaps. 13—28) be the main instrument to implement that principle. The Lukan point is that God is getting ready to move out.

In Luke-Acts there are two main missionary thrusts in the post-Easter period: Acts 2—12 and 13—28. Prior to each there are three prerequisites: (1) a choosing (Luke 6:13 and Acts 1:24; Acts 9:15a); (2) a commissioning (Luke 24:46–49 and Acts 1:8; Acts 9:15b–16; see 22:14–15, 21; 26:16–18); and (3) an indication that the time to move out has arrived (Acts 1:4–5, 8 and chap 2; Acts 13:1–3). Acts 9:1–31 tells of the choice and commissioning of Paul for the missionary outreach of chapters 13—28. The choice and commissioning come through a Christophany. In Mediterranean culture generally, religious vocation was often based on a divine manifestation to the person. For example, in Euripides' *Bacchanals* 469, Dionysius defends his mission to bring a new religion to Greece by claiming it was grounded in a theophany of Zeus. In like manner, Luke says that when God gets ready to move out to the Gentiles, he chooses and commissions his servant through a Christophany.

Three aspects of the surface structure of the unit assist one in clarifying the intent of the narrative. (1) The narrative about Paul's conversion (vss. 1–19) has a formal parallel in 2 Maccabees 3. In both texts (a) an enemy sets out to do an act against God's house or people; (b) there is a divine intervention resulting in the enemy's falling to the ground or being in darkness; (c) a devout person intervenes on the enemy's behalf and he is relieved of his afflictions; and (d) the enemy then becomes a believer in the God who overpowered him and bears witness to him. This is the form of a story about a god overpowering his enemy. Paul's conversion and call are depicted in Acts 9 as a Christophany in which the risen Lord overpowers Saul, the persecutor of the church (9:1; see 8:3).

(2) Acts 9:1–31's action takes place in two geographical locales: Damascus (vss. 1–25) and Jerusalem (vss. 26–30). The section centered at Damascus is chiastically arranged (see John Bligh, *Galatians* [London: St. Paul Publications, 1969], p. 95).

A—Paul plots against the Christians in Damascus (vss. 1–2)

  B—Paul sees the vision, is blinded, and fasts (vss. 3–9)

    C—Ananias sees a vision, is commissioned to go to Paul (vss. 10–14)

      D—Paul's mission is foretold by Christ (vss. 15–16)

    C'—Ananias goes to Paul and reports his vision (vs. 17)

  B'—Paul's sight is restored, he is baptized and eats (vss. 18–19a)

A'—Paul preaches Christ in Damascus, the Jews plot to kill him (vss. 19b–25).

The significance of this surface structure is that its centerpiece focuses the item of central significance for the Evangelist: Paul's commission. "Go, for he is a chosen instrument of mine to carry my name before the Gentiles and kings and the sons of Israel; for I will show him how much he must suffer for the sake of my name." When the risen Christ overpowers Paul, it is in the interest of the mission described here.

(3) There are parallels between the end of the unit centered on Damascus and the entirety of the section with Jerusalem as its locale (see D. Gill, "The Structure of Acts 9," *Biblica*, 55 [1974] pp. 46–48).

Ananias hesitates to believe Paul has been converted (vss. 13–14).	(a) The disciples in Jerusalem fear Paul. They do not believe he is a believer (vs. 26).
The Lord reassures Ananias (vss. 15–16).	(b) Barnabas reassures the Jerusalem Christians (vs. 27).

Ananias goes to Paul and does as he was told (vss. 17–19a); Paul is with the disciples in Damascus (vs. 19b).
Paul preaches immediately in the synagogue (vss. 20–22).

The Jews plot to kill Paul (vss. 23–24).
Paul escapes (vs. 25).

(c) Paul was with them, going in and out among them in Jerusalem (vs. 28a).

(d) Paul speaks freely in the name of the Lord (vss. 28b–29a).

(e) The Hellenistis seek to kill Paul (vs. 29b).

(f) Paul escapes (vs. 30).

The very pattern which makes the narrative repetitious indicates the issue is whether or not Paul's conversion and commissioning were genuine. Ananias and the disciples in Jerusalem doubt it. The narrative functions, however, as a confirmation of Paul's experience in a number of ways: (a) the vision to Ananias (vss. 10–12) with its reassurance (vss. 15–16); (b) Paul's preaching (vss. 20, 22; 28–29) in obedience to the commission of vs. 15; (c) Barnabas' vouching for him (vs. 27); and (d) Paul's sufferings (vss. 23–25; 29–30) in fulfillment of the prophecy of vs. 16. If the first nineteen verses describe the conversion of Paul, what follows functions to confirm the authenticity of that conversion and call (cf. Matt 7:15–20).

In Acts 9:1–31, then, we have a narrative in which the Lord Jesus overpowers his enemy, Paul the persecutor of the church. The Christophany involves both Paul's call to discipleship and his commissioning as a chosen instrument to bear witness. Various means are then employed to give confirmation to the genuineness of Paul's experience. God has a person for every situation. When he gets ready to move out, the Lord goes after his man. Paul's participation in the way is not as a "walk on" but as one overpowered by the summons of his call by Jesus.

From Luke's point of view, the Lord had in Paul a witness fundamentally different from the Twelve. In Luke-Acts there are two kinds of disciples: those "with him" and those not with him. In Luke 8:38–39 the Gerasene demoniac when healed begged Jesus that "he might be with him." But Jesus sent him away, saying: "Return to your home and declare how much God has done for you." In Luke 9:49–50 John asks about a man casting out demons in Jesus name who was not following "with us." These disciples who are not with Jesus are those who have been touched by Jesus in some way but do not accompany him throughout his ministry. By contrast, Luke 8:1; 22:28; 24:44; Acts 1:21–22; 13:31 speak of those who were with Jesus from the baptism of John until his ascension. The Twelve fit into this category; Paul into the camp of those not with him all during his ministry. In Luke-Acts these two types of disciples function symbolically. The Twelve who were with him function as the symbol of the tradition. Those who were not with him, like Paul, bear witness on the basis of their experience (see Acts 26:16). The Twelve who symbolize the tradition were not ready to be God's instruments until they were empowered by an experience. Paul who symbolizes those bearing witness out of vivid experience was not ready to be used by Christ until he was vouched for by the Jerusalem apostles (i.e., his experience was deemed Christian by the tradition). For Luke-Acts it is not either tradition or experience but rather tradition and experience. Both are necessary to enable one to be an adequate witness for the Lord.

Acts 9 can be preached in a variety of ways. Two will be suggested here. One might be entitled "A Call to Ministry." It might open with the observation that when God gets ready to move out, he finds an instrument. This choice of a person for special ministry has often been designated a "call." What does such a "call" involve? H. Richard Niebuhr, *The Purpose of the Church and Its Ministry* (New York: Harper, 1956), pp. 64–65, spoke of such a call being threefold. Acts agrees. First, there is the providential call. Paul in Acts was providentialy educated at the feet of Gamaliel, spoke Aramaic and Greek, and was a Roman citizen. All of these providential gifts enabled him to carry out his mission. Second, there is the private call. Acts 9:1–19 narrates this dimension of the apostles's calling. Third, there is the ecclesiastical call. Acts 9:26–30 focuses on this facet of the Lukan Paul's calling. It is important to note that no one of these dimensions of a "call" to ministry can be omitted if God's tasks are to be carried out.

Another sermon based on this text might be entitled, "Discipleship: Two Types." This sermon would emphasize the conversion dimension of Acts 9 rather than the call aspect. It would build on the Lukan distinction between the Twelve and Paul, those who had been "with him" and the one who had not. In Luke-Acts, the Twelve and Paul symbolize disciples who are identified with the tradition and those who exemplify religious experience. The sermon would focus first on their differences. One type (the Twelve) knew the facts of Jesus' career and then had to come to an experience of God's power. The other type (Paul) began with the experience of God's power and then had to come to live within the tradition. The sermon would then turn to their similarities. Both types eventually came to live out of both tradition and experience. Both types bore witness to Jesus and suffered for him. Such a sermon would allow the Third Evangelist to enable us to see that different people come to Jesus along different routes. What is crucial is that we all get there and that our lives reflect our conversion.

In Step with God (9:32—11:18)

Acts 9:32—11:18 narrates three incidents of evangelization by Peter: (1) 9:32–35; (2) 9:36–43; and (3) 10:1—11:18. (a) These three stories show Peter fulfilling the commisson of the risen Jesus (Acts 1:8—"you shall be my witnesses in . . . all Judea [9:32–35; 9:36–43] . . . and to the end of the earth" [10:1—11:18]) just as the three stories about members of the Seven in Acts 6:8—8:40 show them fulfilling the same injunction ("witnesses in Jerusalem [6:8—7:60] and in . . . Samaria [8:4–13] and to the end of the earth" [8:26–40]). (b) Each of the three Petrine narratives also echoes an event in the career of the earthly Jesus (Acts 9:32–35//Luke 5:18–26; Acts 9:36–43//Luke 8:40–56; Acts 10//Luke 7:2–10), indicating that what the risen Lord commands is in continuity with what the earthly Jesus did (see John 14:12). (c) That two of the Petrine incidents echo the Elijah–Elisha cycles of the OT (Acts 9:36–43//1 Kings 17; 2 Kings 4; Acts 10//2 Kings 5) argues that the apostle's actions are scripturally based. (d) Moreover, each of the three stories about Peter's witness has a parallel in the narrative about Paul later in Acts (9:32–35//14:8–12; 9:36–43//20:7–12; 10:1—11:18// chaps. 13—28), implying that Paul's mission did not deviate from that of his Jewish-Christian predecessors. There is a unity of Christian practice. All of these devices are Lukan attempts to legitimate what the apostle Peter is doing.

The first two stories (Acts 9:32–35; 9:36–43) have a dual function within the Lukan narrative, the one literary the other theological. On the theological level, Acts 9:32–43 continues the theme that miracle may serve as a catalyst for faith (9:35; 9:42b; see Luke 4:31—5:11). For the Evangelist miracle may not always produce faith; it is not compelling proof (Luke 17:11–17). But when it does evoke faith, that faith is as genuine as that evoked by other means. On the literary level, these two stories serve to bring Peter to Joppa (9:43), just south of Caesarea, so he can be reached easily by Cornelius' messengers (10:1, 7–8).

The third story (10:1—11:18) is the crucial one for Luke. Its importance is seen in the repetition involved. First the events are narrated (chap 10), then they are recounted (11:1–18). Later they will be recalled (15:7–11, 14). Like the threefold repetition of the account of Paul's conversion (Acts 9; 22; 26), this reiteration is for emphasis. Here the Evangelist legitimates the principle of the movement to the Gentiles. Two separate problems have to be dealt with in establishing the Gentile mission's legitimacy. On the one hand, there is the question of the clean-unclean laws (10:28; 11:3; see Lev 11). One obstacle to a mission to Gentiles is that it brings Jews who follow the laws of purity into contact with people whose person and food are reckoned unclean. On the other hand, there is the matter of whether or not God wants the Gentiles included at this point in time (10:44–48; 11:1, 18; see Isa 2:1–4; Tobit 14:5–7 where Gentiles are included but not until the End). Acts 10:1—11:18 focuses on both of these issues.

In order to see clearly what the author is doing in Acts 10:1—11:18, one needs to understand the surface structure. The unit begins with a double vision, similar to that in Acts 9:1–19: (1) the vision of Cornelius and its message (10:1–8), and (2) the vision of Peter and its interpretation (10:9–16, 17–20). Then there follows a unit of recollection in an ABA' pattern.

A—Recollection of the vision to Cornelius (vs. 22)
        B—Recollection of the vision to Peter (vss. 28–29)
A'—Recollection of the vision to Cornelius (vss. 30–33).

To this point the story is concerned with the problem of the purity laws.

In the double vision scene (10:1–8, 9–21) both Cornelius and Peter are praying (vss. 2–3, 30; 9). In this context God communicates with each. This is in line with the Lukan belief that prayer is the means by which God makes his will known for new departures in the unfolding of his plan for history (see Luke 3:21–22; 6:12–16; 9:18–22; 9:28–31; 22:39–46; Acts 1:14; 13:1–3). What is communicated to Peter is that the clean-unclean laws of Judaism do not apply so as to block associations with Gentiles who are seeking God. "What God has cleansed, you must not call common" (vs. 15; see Rom 14:14; Mark 7:15; 1 Tim 4:1–4). "Rise and go down, and accompany them without hesitation; for I have sent them" (vs. 20). Obediently Peter first invites the Gentile messengers in to be his guests (vs. 23a), then accompanies them to Cornelius' house (vss. 23b, 25, 27), and finally apparently stays with them some days (vs. 48b). In his disregard of the Jewish laws of purity in the interests of making disciples, Peter acted in a way not only obedient to the heavenly vision but also faithful to what the earthly Jesus had foreshadowed (Luke 5:12–15; 5:29–32; 7:36–50; 10:29–37; 11:37–41; 15:1–2; 19:1–10). Again, religious experience and tradition agree in determining the conduct of Jesus' disciples. They agree that Jewish laws of purity cannot stand in the way of the unfolding of God's plan.

When Peter enters Cornelius' house, the centurion "fell down at his feet and worshiped him" (vs. 25). But Peter will not tolerate this any more than will Paul later (14:11–15). He says to Cornelius: "Stand up; I too am a man" (vs. 26). Although the clean–unclean laws are suspended, the scriptural prohibition against idolatry is not (Exod 20:3). The Lukan evangelists do not draw attention to themselves but to the Lord they represent (vss. 25–26).

In what follows, the focus shifts to the matter of the admission of the Gentiles into the people of God (10:34–48). This section falls into two parts: (1) the speech of Peter (vss. 34–43) and (2) the gift of the Holy Spirit (vss. 44–48). (1) The speech of Peter begins: "Truly I perceive that God shows no partiality, but *in every nation any one* who fears him and does what is right is acceptable to him" (vss. 34–35). It ends on the same note: "To him all the prophets bear witness that *every one* who believes in him receives forgiveness of sins through his name" (vs. 43). This picks up the theme of the universal outreach of the gospel that runs throughout Luke-Acts (e.g., Luke 2:29–32; 3:6; 4:25–27; 24:47—"that repentance and forgiveness of sins should be preached in his name to all nations"; Acts 1:8).

(2) While Peter was still speaking, "the Holy Spirit fell on all who heard the word" (vs. 44). Peter's speech asserting the universal applicability of the name of Jesus is proved true by the events that transpired. The risen Christ poured out (vs. 45—see 2:17, 33) the Spirit even on the Gentiles. The Jewish Christians ("those from the circumcised"—vs. 45) accompanying Peter were amazed. Peter's response was that if God had so obviously included the Gentiles, the church's reception of them must follow. "Can anyone forbid water for baptizing these people who have received the Holy Spirit just as we have?" (vs. 47). He then commands them to be baptized. By the initiating act of the Lord and the responsive act of the apostle, the Gentiles are included in the people of God.

Acts 11:1–18 tells of an evaluation by the church in Jerusalem of what had transpired in Caesarea. The question raised by the Jewish Christians (vs. 2—"those from the circumcision," as in 10:45, not "the circumcision party" as in the RSV) has to do with the question of Jewish laws of purity. "Why did you go to uncircumcised men and eat with them?" (vs. 3). Peter's orderly response answers that question in vss. 5–13: (1) Peter had a vision, and (2) Cornelius had a similar one. Peter says he went in obedience to a divine command. Having answered the specific question about purity, the apostle moves on to the further issue, that of the legitimacy of the Gentiles in the people of God (vss. 14–17). The arguments are three. First, Cornelius' vision told him that he and his household would be saved (vs. 14). Second, the Holy Spirit fell on Cornelius and the others just as he had on the Jewish Christians in Acts 2 (vs. 15). Third, this experience fulfilled the words of the Lord about being baptized with the Holy Spirit (vs. 16; see Acts 1:4–5). From this evidence Peter draws his conclusion. "If then God gave the same gift to them as he gave to us when we believed in the Lord Jesus Christ, who was I that I could withstand God?" (vs. 17). There follows the climax to the entire unit: "Then to the Gentiles also God has granted repentence unto life" (vs. 18b). The church deems right what God's acts so indicate.

This passage that is so important to the Lukan narrative yields a sermon that may be entitled, "In Step with God." In beginning one may note that our cultural and religious contexts often obscure for us what God has spoken through his Son. Only a closeness to God, enabled by prayer, facilitates our vision of God's will, permitting us to "move on in step" with what we see God is doing in practice in the world. This is precisely the case with Peter in Acts 10—11.

On the one hand, it took a private word to enable Peter to catch up in attitude with what God wanted (10:9–20; 11:5–12). Note first that Peter's experience was in discontinuity with his cultural-religious predisposition. Through Peter's experience, the communication was initially given in principle (10:9–16), then in a particular situation (10:19–20). Note also that Peter's experience was in continuity with what was foreshadowed in the life of the earthly Jesus.

On the other hand, it took a public demonstration to enable Peter to keep up with what God was doing (10:44–48; 11:15–17). Note first that Peter's experience was discontinuous with past practice and theory. Note also that Peter's experience was in continuity with the word of the risen Lord (11:16; 1:4–5).

In conclusion, we may note that profound religious experience related both to prayer and to public demonstration can cause Christians to see and hear in Jesus Christ something obscured by cultural-religious tradition. Having understood, one can get in step and keep in step with what God is doing and wants to do in the world (see John 15:26b; 16:13a, 14–15).

A Man for the Moment (11:19–30; 12:25)

Acts 11:19–30 is a brief narrative unit about the origins of the Gentile congregation in Antioch of Syria. Virtually every sentence reflects some major Lukan concern. It would be well to look at the parts before making an assessment of the whole.

(1) Vs. 19, "Now those who were scattered because of the persecution that arose over Stephen," resumes the thread of 8:1–4: "they were all scattered. . . . Now those who were scattered went about preaching the word." Whereas Acts 8 told

of preaching in Samaria and to the Ethiopian eunuch, Acts 11:19–21 speaks of preaching that reached even to Gentiles in Antioch. Luke again makes the point that persecution spreads the gospel.

(2) Vss. 20–21 indicate that in Antioch, as elsewhere, the success of the Christian mission depends on a dual witness: that of the disciples (vs. 20) and the hand of the Lord (vs. 21—(see 4:30; 5:32; 14:3). From the Lukan perspective, without the twofold witness there would not have been "a great number . . . that turned to the Lord."

(3) In vs. 22 ("News of this came to the ears of the church in Jerusalem, and they sent Barnabas to Antioch"), there are three Lukan threads that need unravelling. First, there is evident here the motif of the Jerusalem supervision of the missionary outreach in Acts. In Acts 8:14–17, after Philip had evangelized the Samaritans, Jerusalem sent Peter and John to complete the process. In 9:26–30 Paul's conversion is legitimated by the Jerusalem Christians. Acts 11:1–18 tells how even Peter was accountable to the Jerusalem church after his visit to the house of Cornelius. In 15:1–35 the various dimensions of Paul's missionary work in chapters 13–14 are debated and approved by Jerusalem. On Paul's missionary travels he is accompanied by Jerusalem Christians: Barnabas and Silas. After each journey Paul returns to Jerusalem. The significance of this Lukan pattern is that Jerusalem is the center where the Twelve reside. Remember that even in the persecution after Stephen's martyrdom the apostles did not leave the city (8:1b). Furthermore, the Twelve are those who were with the earthly Jesus from his baptism by John until his ascension (Acts 1:21–22). They know the true facts of the gospel history. As such they are witnesses to the people (Acts 1:22; 5:32; 10:41; 13:31). The Twelve, then, stand for the true tradition about Jesus. Their witness is the norm for what is truly Christian. Jerusalem control means the control of the spreading Christian experience by the tradition of the earthly Jesus. That a Jerusalem delegate, Barnabas, is dispatched to Antioch is Luke's way of saying that this Gentile religious experience needs to be examined to make sure it stands within the boundaries of what is truly Christian. "When he came and saw the grace of God, he was glad; and he exhorted them all to remain faithful to the Lord with steadfast purpose" (vs. 23).

Second, it is the intent of the Lukan narrative to show the mission to the Gentiles in Antioch and its approval by Barnabas as an extension of Acts 10:1—11:18. After the examination of Peter in 11:1–18, the Jerusalem Christians had approved, in principle, his evangelization of Cornelius. "Then to the Gentiles also God has granted repentance unto life" (vs. 18b). Once this principle is established, the narrative tells of its implementation on a grand scale by others (11:19–24). That Barnabas would be positive in his evaluation is to be expected by Luke's readers given the Jerusalem church's decision in 11:18.

Third, Barnabas' approval of a Gentile Christian congregation is to be expected given Luke's description of him: "full of the Holy Spirit" (vs. 24). In Acts 1:8, the risen Jesus had said that his disciples would be witnesses to the ends of the earth after they had experienced the Holy Spirit (see Luke 24:47–49). In Lukan theology, the gift of the Spirit is the experiential base from which the mission to all nations takes off.

(4) Vss. 25–26 tell how Barnabas went to Tarsus to get Saul, to bring him to Antioch, and to enlist his aid in the nurture of the new Christians. Again, three Lukan emphases can be discerned. First, in Acts evangelization is followed by nurture. Acts 2:42 says that after the Pentecostal ingathering, "they devoted themselves to the apostles' teaching and fellowship, to the breaking of bread and the prayers." Acts 4:23–35 also tells of their corporate worship and sharing. So here, Barnabas and Saul meet with the church and teach.

Second, now for the third time in the narrative of Acts one meets the necessity to add new leadership so as to be able to perform the tasks at hand (1:15–26; 6:1–6). Having confidence in Paul's conversion and call (9:27), Barnabas enlisted him to help.

Third, just as Acts showed the Jerusalem church confirm the authenticity of Paul's conversion due to Barnabas' advocacy (9:26–30), now their delegate to Antioch, Barnabas, includes Paul in his work with the developing Gentile church in Antioch (11:25–26). Paul's ministry is now confirmed on the initiative of a Jerusalem-approved leader (see the *Epistle of the Apostles*, 31, for a similar view of Paul's apostleship in relation to the Twelve). Not only is the mission approved, the missionary is also.

(5) Vss. 27–30 give a demonstration of the unity of Gentile and Jewish Christians in the one people of God as evidenced by the sharing of material possessions. The backdrop of this expression of fellowship is the prophecy of Agabus that there would be a famine under Claudius. When the Evangelist says "this took place in the days of Claudius" (vs. 28), he is probably referring to the famine in Judea in A.D. 46–47 when queen Helena of Adiabene sent corn to relieve the hunger among the poor in Jerusalem (Josephus, *Antiquities*, 3:15:3; 20:2:5; 20:5:2; see Suetonius, "Claudius," 19; Tacitus, *Annals*, 12:43). In any case, the fulfillment of Agabus' prophecy here reinforces the seriousness of his prediction later in Acts 21:10–11.

The Evangelist gives a two-sided portrayal of wealth. On the one side, he depicts it in negative terms. Acts 1:18 says Judas' betrayal of Jesus was for money. In 5:1–11, Ananias and Sapphira lie to the Holy Spirit because of money. Simon the magician seeks the ability to impart the Holy Spirit by the laying on of hands in exchange for money (Acts 8:18). In 16:16–24, the Philippian owners of a divining slave girl cause Paul and Silas to be thrown into prison over their loss of gain. Acts 19:23–41 tells how the silversmiths in Ephesus riot over the threat to their income. Felix, in 24:26, keeps Paul in prison in hopes that he will be given a bribe. Throughout Acts the author says in effect that a concern for money to the point of valuing it above all else is a primary trait of a godless world (see Luke 18:19ff; 16:18ff; 12:1ff; see 1 Tim 6:10; Polycarp, *To the Philippians*, 4:1).

On the other side, the Lukan evangelist can sometimes depict wealth in positive terms. Private property is assumed (Acts 2:45; 4:37; 5:4). Nevertheless, property ownership and rights are subordinated to human need within the community of disciples. Since property is an extension of one's personality, to commit oneself to others within a community involves the sharing of wealth. That this happened in Jerusalem (Acts 2:44–45; 4:32, 34, 35, 36–37; 6:1–6), Luke believed fulfilled the hopes of the Jews and the ideals of the Greeks.

In Acts 11:27–30 the Gentile Christians in Antioch are shown acting in the same way that the new converts in Jerusalem had acted earlier. They share their material goods, however, not with one another but with the Jewish Christians in Jerusalem. In this way they demonstrate their full participation in the church of the apostles and testify to the unity of Jews and Gentiles within the Christian fellowship (see Eph 2:11–22). It is significant, moreover, that when the Antiochian Christians act in this way, they are behaving like their teacher, Barnabas (Acts 4:36–37): "like teacher, like disciple" (Luke 6:40).

Any assessment of Acts 11:19–30 as a whole must see it within its larger context. The movement of the narrative of Acts 8—11 is like waves of an incoming tide, each pushing ahead towards the ultimate limit. So in chapter 8 the word goes first to the Samaritans and then to the Ethiopian eunuch. In chapter 10 Cornelius is included. Now in Acts 11 many Gentiles are incorporated along with the converted Jews in the church at Antioch. The principle is firmly established: (1) Gentiles are included in the fellowship; (2) Jews and Gentiles can associate with one another in the church. The stage is set. The missionary has been called and legitimated. It only remains for God to say when the time to move out has come.

This is a good time to develop a sermon on Barnabas. It might be called, "A Man for the Moment." Note that a principle has been etablished. Its applicability is now being tested. Strains are bound to result. Will the church be able to stand by its principles and still stay together? In such a time the right person is needed: one who can be a bridge person. Such a person is Barnabas. He is a man for the moment because of his timely gifts. First, he was accepted in the established body (4:36–37) because of his wealth and generosity. Second, he was acceptable to the innovators from Cyprus and Cyrene (11:20) because he was from Cyprus (4:36). Third, he was open to God and his leading, being full of the Spirit (11:24). Fourth, he was open to the inclusion of new blood in the church, vouching for Saul (9:27). Fifth, he was apparently patient with the young and untried, as exemplified in his attitude toward Mark (12:25; 13:13; 15:37–40). Sixth, he was sensitive to what was appropriate, recognizing the sharing of possessions as a sign of Christian unity (11:29–30; see 2:45; 4:34–35). Barnabas could not have done what Peter did (10:1—11:18); he could not do what only Paul would be able to do (chaps. 13—28); but he was the man for the moment—

to make the transition from Peter's establishment of the principle to Paul's universal application of it. He was God's person for the moment, to uphold the hard-won principle and
maintain the crucial unity of the fellowship.

The Word of God and the State (12:1–24)

This section, Acts 12:1–24, is composed of two stories
about Herod: (1) Herod Agrippa's hostility toward the church
(vss. 1–19), and (2) his hostility toward the people of Tyre and
Sidon (vss. 20–23). Its conclusion is: "But the word of God
grew and multiplied" (vs. 24). These stories make two points:
(1) unrighteous rulers cannot stop the progress of the gospel
(vss. 1–19); and (2) rulers who try to usurp the place of God
will be judged (vss. 20–23). Together they affirm that the
progress of the gospel is unstoppable.

Acts 12:1–19 speaks of Herod's hostility to the church in
two stages: (1) he killed James, the son of Zebedee (vs. 2); and
(2) he arrested and imprisoned Peter (vss. 3–5a). The narrative about Peter is told as a miracle story: (a) the problem:
imprisonment (vss. 3–5a); (b) the solution: prayer (vs. 5b)
and its answer (vss. 6–12); (c) the reactions to the miracle:
first by the Christians (vss. 13–17) and then by the non-Christians (vss. 18–19). This particular type of miracle story is
found elsewhere in Acts: e.g., Acts 5:17–21, where the apostles are freed from the common prison ("But at night an angel of the Lord opened the prison doors and brought them
out"), and Acts 16:25–28, where Paul and Silas experience
the opening of the prison doors and the unfastening of their
fetters.

This type of miracle story belongs to a Gattung of escape
legends known both in Greco-Roman and in Jewish circles in
antiquity. From the Greek world we may mention Euripides'
The Bacchae, 443–48, which tells of the escape of some
maidens who had succumbed to Dionysian madness.

> The captured Bacchanals you put in ward,
> And in the common prison bound with chains;
> Fled to the meadows are they, loosed from bonds,
> And dance and call on Bromius the god.
> The fetters from their feet self-sundered fell;
> Doors, without mortal hand, unbarred themselves.

Similar stories from the Greco Roman world are found in

Philostratus' *Life of Apollonius of Tyana*, 7:38, and in Ovid's *Metamorphoses*, 3:695ff. A Jewish tradition of similar nature is found in Artapanus' story of Moses. Artapanus in his book *Concerning the Jews* (reported by Eusebius, *The Preparation for the Gospel*, 9:27) says that the Egyptian Pharaoh shut Moses up in prison. "But when it was night, all the doors of the prison-house opened of their own accord, and of the guards some died, and some were sunk in sleep, and their weapons broken in pieces. So Moses passed out and came to the palace." Such stories of liberaton were told to say that there is nothing that can prevent the god and his followers from conquering the world. The author of Luke-Acts has appropriated this form to tell of several deliverances of the missionaries in early Christian history with the same aim. Here in Acts 12 the point is clear. The power of the State is impotent to stop the gospel (12:24).

Acts 12:20–23, which speaks of Herod's hostility towards the people of Tyre and Sidon, is a variant of a similar tradition found in Josephus' *Antiquities*, 19:8:2. As Josephus tells it, at a festival in Caesarea Agrippa put on a garment made entirely of silver and came into the theater in the morning. When the sun hit it, it shone marvelously. Flatterers cried out that he was a god: "although we have hitherto reverenced you only as a man, yet shall we henceforth regard you as superior to mortal nature." The king did not rebuke them or reject their flattery. He then saw a bird of ill omen. A severe pain arose in his stomach. He then said: "I, whom you call a god, am commanded presently to depart this life; while Providence reproves the lying words you just now said to me. And I, who was by you called immortal, am immediately to be hurried away by death." After five days, he died. Josephus' account differs from that in Acts in several ways. (1) In Acts the occasion was a delegation from Tyre and Sidon; in Josephus it was a festival in honor of Caesar. (2) In Acts Herod's oration brings acclamation; in Josephus it was the sun's reflection off of his silver garment. (3) In Acts Herod is eaten by worms; in Josephus he dies of a pain in his stomach. The two accounts are similar in that both attribute Herod's death to his not rejecting the acclamation of his divinity.

This story belongs to a Gattung with a long history in Jewish circles. It speaks of the divine humiliation of the person

who pretends to be God. A very similar narrative is found in
2 Maccabees 9. This passage tells how Antiochus' insolence
in thinking that he was more than human was judged by God
who struck him an incurable blow. He was seized with a pain
in his bowels (vs. 5) and his body swarmed with worms (vs.
9). Before he died he acknowledged: "It is right to be subject
to God, and no mortal should think that he is equal to God"
(vs. 12). The OT prototype is found in Ezek 28:1–10 and Isa
14:12–20. In Isa 14 there is a taunt against the king of
Babylon:

> (13) You have said in your heart, "I will ascend to
>   heaven"
> (14) "I will make myself like the Most High."
> (15) But you are brought down to Sheol, to the depths of
>   the Pit.

In Ezek 28 we hear of the king of Tyre:

> (2) Because your heart is proud, and you have said, "I am
>   a god"
> (6) Because you consider yourself as wise as a god
> (7) Therefore
> (8) you will die.
> (9) Will you still say, "I am a god," in the presence of
>   those who will slay you?

Both the kings of Tyre and Babylon are cast down because,
although men, they exalt themselves above human measure.
This Gattung has as its point that God will not allow anyone,
even the greatest ruler, to usurp his place. He humbles the
exalted (see Luke 14:11; Prov 3:34; James 4:6; 1 Pet 5:5). The
author of Luke-Acts uses this form of story to make a similar
point: rulers who try to usurp the place of God will be
judged.

This passage needs to be considered in light of the total
Lukan attitude towards the State. Overall Luke-Acts is positively disposed towards the State (e.g., Luke 7:1–10; Acts
13:4–12; 18:12–17; 19:23–41; 23:10; 23:12–33; 26:32;
27:42–43). Even when Roman officials fall below acceptable
standards of behavior, the system of Roman justice is viewed
favorably (e.g., Acts 16:19–39; 17:1–9; 22:22–29; 24:26—25:2;
see Pilate's recognition of Jesus' innocence before suc-

cumbing to Jewish pressure in Luke 23). Most often the Roman judicial system protected the apostles from chaos and caprice of an unruly mob. In this positive attitude towards the State, the Evangelist agrees with a major stream of early Christian thinkers (e.g., Rom 13:1–7; 1 Tim 2:1–6; 1 Pet 2:13–14; 1 Clement 60:4—61:1; Polycarp, *To the Philippians*, 12:3). This stance echoes the sentiments of the early rabbis: "Pray for the welfare of the government, for were it not for the fear of it, men would swallow one another alive" (*Pirke Aboth*, 3:2).

Acts 12, however, is critical of rulers who exalt themselves to the place of God and who act hostilely towards the church. In this critical attitude Luke agrees with yet another stream of early Christian thought (e.g., Revelation; Barnabas 4:2–4; Sibylline Oracle 4:117–18). Both of these attitudes, positive and negative, have their roots in the logion of the Lukan Jesus (Luke 20:25): "Render to Caesar the things that are Caesar's, and to God the things that are God's." Luke-Acts has the most balanced view of the State in the New Testament. It contains both poles of early Christian thought, positive and negative. In Acts 12 the Evangelist says: neither the State's hostility towards Christians nor its ruler's exaltation of himself to a godlike position can stay the triumph of the gospel.

This text can serve as a partial basis for a sermon on "The Word of God and the State." The question to be addressed by the Lukan Evangelist is: How should Christians regard the State? The answer provided by Luke-Acts is twofold: (1) with appreciation, and (2) with confidence. Christians should regard the State with appreciation because, for the most part, the State assists in the furthering of the gospel; with confidence because, even when not on our side, the State cannot stop the progress of the gospel. On the one hand, the State, for the most part, is on our side in furthering the gospel. In general this is true because the State protects Christians from chaos. In particular circumstances, when its representatives are unworthy, it is still true because the system itself is helpful. On the other hand, the State, even when it is not on our side, cannot stop the gospel. To would-be enemies Acts says: individual Christians may suffer (vss. 1–2) but the spread of the gospel is unstoppable (vss. 3–17, 24). To would-be deities Acts issues a warning: there is one God, the Creator (vss. 23b), who humbles the exalted (vss. 20–23a). In conclusion, it is important that we, like the Third Evangelist, appreciate the benefits the Christian movement derives from the State at the same time that we confidently assert that even if the State were not helpful, it would be impotent to stymie the word of God (12:24).

The Commission Fulfilled: Stage Two
(Acts 13:1—28:31)

A Portrait of Conversion (13:1—14:28)

This section is one large thought unit, analogous to Acts 10:1—11:18. There is an Antioch frame around it; the missionary work of Barnabas and Paul moves out from Antioch and returns there (13:1-3, departure from Antioch; 14:26–28, return to Antioch). Acts 14:27 also echoes 13:2 where the prophetic word refers to "the work to which I have called them." This is an additional bracket around the unit. Just as 1:8 has the risen Jesus give the commission to the apostles and chapter 10 has the vision and the Spirit speak to the specifics of the case, with the result that Peter goes to the Gentiles, so 9:15–16 has the risen Christ give Paul's commission as 13:1–4 has the Spirit speak to the specific task, with the result that Paul goes to the Gentiles. Just as the climax of 10:1—11:18 was stated in 11:18b ("Then to the Gentiles also God has granted repentance unto life"), so the climax of chapters 13—14 comes in 14:27 (God "had opened a door of faith to the Gentiles").

Acts 13—14 functions as a fulfillment of all three of the components of Paul's commission stated in Acts 9:15–16. "He is a chosen instrument of mine to carry my name (1) before the Gentiles and kings and (2) the sons of Israel; for (3) I will show him how much he must suffer for the sake of my name"— (1) before the Gentiles (14:27; 13:7–12; 13:46–48; 14:8–18); (2) and the sons of Israel (13:14–41); (3) he must suffer (14:5, 19; cf. 2 Tim 3:10–11; 2 Cor 11:24–25).

The narrative of Acts 13—14 moves out from Antioch to Salamis (13:5), to Paphos (13:6–13a), to Perga (13:13b), to Antioch of Pisidia (13:14–51a), to Iconium (14:1–5), to Lystra (14:6–20a), and finally to Derbe (14:20b–21a). Then there is a brief retracing of steps to Lystra, Iconium, Antioch of Pisidia, Perga (14:21b–25), and from there a return to Antioch of Syria (14:26–28). Within the itinerary there are three major narrative sections: (1) Paphos (13:6–13a) where the missionaries encounter a certain magician, Bar-Jesus; (2) Antioch of Pisidia (13:14–51a) where Paul speaks out at length to the synagogue; and (3) Lystra (14:6–20a) where Barnabas and Paul are acclaimed gods after the healing of a lame man. The other parts of Acts 13—14 have the nature of summary material. It would seem that if one wished to hear where the author wanted the emphasis placed in his narrative about the movement to the Gentiles, attention ought to be focused on these three major sections. Their pattern is ABA': A—miracle in a pagan context, B—preaching in a Jewish setting, A'—miracle in a pagan milieu.

Acts 13:1–3 is the base upon which the missionary journey rests. This paragraph indicates that the outreach to follow happens at God's initiative through a word of prophecy: "Set apart for me Barnabas and Saul for the work to which I have called them" (vs. 22). The Spirit leads the church to confirm the call the two missionaries had already received. It is, therefore, possible for the Evangelist to say both that the church "sent them off" (vs. 3) and that they were "sent out by the Holy Spirit" (vs. 4). This divine initiative is reaffirmed at the end of the journey when Paul and Barnabas "declared all that God had done with them" (14:27). As elsewhere in Acts, the mission is God's doing.

Acts 13:6–13a, the first of the three major incidents of chapters 13—14, tells of an encounter between the missionaries and a Jewish magician and false prophet, Elymas or Bar-Jesus. Such court astrologers who predicted the future and claimed to be able to alter fate with their magic were not uncommon in Roman circles. For example, Suetonius' biography of Nero tells of some astrologers predicting to Nero his repudiation by the Roman people while others prophesied his rule of the East, a few expressly naming the sovereignty of Jerusalem. The encounter is depicted in terms of a miracle story: (1) the problem: Elymas sought to turn the proconsul of Paphos away from Christianity (vs. 8); (2) the miracle; the magician is rendered temporarily blind (vss. 9-11); (3) the result: the proconsul believed (vs. 12). Miracle, in Luke-Acts is often a catalyst for faith (Luke 4:31—5:11; Acts 9:32–43).

It is a particular type of miracle story, that of a contest between God's representative and that of other alleged powers (e.g., 1 Kings 18:19–40, the contest of Elijah with the prophets of Baal on Mount Carmel; Acts of Peter 23—28, the contest of Peter and Simon the magician in the forum before the Roman officials). The purpose of this type of miracle story is to indicate that there is one true and living God and that all other claims are counterfeit. This is certainly the way it functions here. As a result of the Holy Spirit's working through him in this way (vs. 9), Paul emerges into the prominent role (compare 11:30; 12:25; 13:2, 7 with 13:13!). It is God who decides on leadership just as it is he who decides on the mission and the missionaries.

Acts 13:14a–51a, the second of the three major incidents of the missionary journey, narrates two synagogue scenes in Antioch of Pisidia. (1) The first is 13:14b–43. This unit is framed by "they went into the synagogue" (vs. 14) and "they went out" (vs. 42). There is a brief narrative to set the stage for the speech (vs. 15) and a short account of the effects of the speech (vss. 42–43). The speech itself falls into three parts, signaled by the threefold address (vss. 16b, 26, 38a; see Luke 6:20, 27, 39). The synagogue service is described in a way similar to that in Philo (*De spec leg* 2:62). The first part of the speech (vss. 16b–25) shows that Jesus is of David's posterity and is the fulfillment of God's promises (see Rom 1:3). The second part of the speech (vss. 26–37) shows both the human rejection of Jesus in the cross and the divine affirmation of him in the resurrection (see Rom 1:4). The third part (vss. 38–41) states that through Jesus forgiveness and deliverance (literally, justification; see Rom 6:7) are available and warns against unbelief (see Acts 2:38; 10:43).

(2) The second synagogue scene and its aftermath (vss. 44–51a) consist of two parallel units detailing the results of the preaching.

A— The whole city gathered to hear the word (vs. 44).
 B— The Jews reject it (vs. 45).
  C— Paul turns to the Gentiles (vss. 46–47).
   D— The Gentiles are glad (vs. 48).
A'— The word spread throughout all the region (vs. 49).
 B'— The Jews stir up persecution (vs. 50).
  C'— Paul shakes off the dust from his feet (vs. 51; see Luke 9:5; 10:11).
   D'— The disciples are filled with joy (vs. 52).

In this second major incident, the Jews who reject the gospel are cast into the camp with Bar-Jesus, while the Jews, the god-fearers, and the Gentiles who believe are grouped with the proconsul of Paphos.

In Acts 14:8–18, the third of the three major incidents of the missionary journey of Acts 13—14, we find another miracle story: (a) the ailment (vs. 8); (b) the cure (vss. 9–10); the reaction (vss. 11–13). In the description of the ailment and the cure (a lame man made to walk), this story echoes Luke 5:18–26; Acts 3:1–10; 9:32–35. This shows that Paul has the same powers as Jesus and Peter before him. It is the same Spirit that empowers all three. The third ingredient, the reaction to the cure, is considerably expanded in order to occasion the apostolic speech on vss. 14–18.

The background for the Lystrans' attribution of divinity to Barnabas and Paul (see 10:25; 28:6) and their attempt to offer sacrifices to them lies in Greek belief generally and Lystran tradition in particular. Greek belief generally is evidenced by Homer's *Odyssey*, 17:485ff.: "For holy gods, in the form of wandering foreigners, taking on various forms, often go through countries and cities, that they may see mortals' foolish misdeeds as well as piety." More particularly, the background is the tale told by Ovid, *Metamorphoses*, 8:631ff., of Zeus and Hermes visiting this region, being entertained by an aged couple, Philemon and Baucis, while the rest of the populace was wiped out for their lack of hospitality. Archeological evidence for the cult of the two gods, dating from about the third century A.D., has been found near Lystra. If the locals had failed to honor the gods on their previous visit, they were anxious to do their duty now. The priest of Zeus starts to offer sacrifice to the apostles (vs. 13). When the apostles tear their garments (vs. 14), it is an expression of horror at any attempt to regard men as divine (see 12:23). This misguided reaction to the miracle occasions the missionaries' speech of vss. 15–17. When they call for the Lystrans to "turn from these vain things to a living God who made the heaven and the earth" (vs. 15b), they are echoing the kerygma of the Hellenistic church (see 1 Thess 1:9–10; 1 Cor 8:6; Acts 17:22–31). In this way, Luke emphasizes the apostolic rejection of pagan idolatry and affirmation of monotheism.

Taken as a whole, Acts 13—14 portrays what is involved in conversion. The three major incidents, 13:6–13a; 13:14–52; 14:8–18, detail the various facets of it. This passage could yield a sermon entitled, "A Portrait of Conversion." Any introduction should make clear that conversion involves both a turning from something and a turning to someone (Jacques Dupont, "Conversion in the Acts of the Apostles," in *The Salvation of the Gentiles* [New York: Paulist, 1979], pp. 61–84) on the one hand, conversion involves turning from something. This involves a turning from all attempts to control the numinous world (13:6–12); from multiple centers of value, all at the human level (14:15); from religious and moral self-sufficiency (13:39b). Jewish rejection of the gospel in 13:45, 14:1–7, and 14:19–23 symbolizes for Luke the human rejection of the suggestion that we are not sufficient to all that is required. On the other hand, conversion involves a turning to someone. It is a turning to the good Creator (14:15, 17); to submission to his will (13:6–12); and to trust in Jesus (13:38–39) for both forgiveness (vs. 38) and deliverance from our bondages (vs. 39). Conversion as dramatized in the journey of Acts 13—14 involves renunciation of magic and the occult, of polytheism, and of legalism. It also involves a monotheistic orientation to life, one in which we do God's will instead of trying to use him to do ours, and one in which we are totally dependent on Jesus for both our acceptance and our ability to do God's will.

When Missionaries Cause Trouble Back Home (15:1–35)

Acts 15:1–35 is a thought unit whose boundaries are signalled by Paul and Barnabas going to Jerusalem (vss. 2, 4) and their going down to Antioch (vss. 30, 35). The surface structure of the unit falls into three parts: (1) the occasion (vss. 1–5); (2) the Council (vss. 6–29); and (3) the outcome (vss. 30–35). Each of these three parts merits examination before attention is directed to the function of the whole in the narrative of Acts.

(1) The pattern of vss. 1–5, the occasion, is ABCB'A'.

A— Men from Judea teach that circumcision is necessary
for salvation (vs. 1).
B— Paul and Barnabas are appointed to go up to Jeru-
salem about the question (vs. 2).
C— On their way they report the conversion of the
Gentiles, bringing joy to the brethren (vs. 3).
B'— When they came to Jerusalem, they were wel-
comed by the church (vs. 4).
A'— Some of the Christian Pharisees said that circumci-
sion and keeping the law is necessary (vs. 5).

The occasion is the claim of some that Gentile Christians, including those at Antioch, if they are to be Christians, must
first become Jews. Only keeping the law will result in salvation (vs. 1—see 11:14; 15:11). Since this runs counter to the
experience of Paul, Barnabas, and the church at Antioch
(11:19–30), it needs to be settled in Jerusalem. The stage is
set for the Council.

(2) The account of the Council is found in vss. 6–29. This narrative consists of two components: (a) the presentation of the
evidence (vss. 7–15), and (b) the proposal and implementation
of a plan (vss. 19–29). (a) The evidence is presented in three
stages. First, Peter speaks (vss. 7–11). His remarks allude to the
Cornelius episode (10:1—11:18). God "made no distinction between us and them, but cleansed (see 10:15) their hearts by
faith" (vs. 9). The conclusion is striking: "we believe that we
shall be saved through the grace of the Lord Jesus, just as they
will" (vs. 11). The implication is that Peter has learned from the
Cornelius episode the basis for his own salvation. "If those who
did not keep the Law were saved by grace, then that must be
the basis of his being saved, who had only with difficulty borne
the Law" (Luke T. Johnson, *Decision Making in the Church*
[Philadelphia: Fortress, 1983], p. 82). Second, Barnabas and
Paul relate "what signs and wonders God had done through
them among the Gentiles" (vs. 12; see 14:3; 4:30; 5:32). Like
Peter, they appeal to experience, simply reporting what had
happened (see 15:3). Third, James takes the floor. He recalls
Peter's dealings with Cornelius, calling the events of chapter 10
a visitation of God (see Luke 19:44). He then says, "With this
the words of the prophets agree" (vs. 15), not, "This agrees with
the prophets." The OT is illuminated and interpreted by ...

God's activity in the present." "James decided for God rather than for precedent" (Johnson, *Decision Making in the Church*, p. 84). The passage to which James appeals is Amos 9:11–12, LXX, a text quoted in the Dead Sea Scrolls (CD 7:16; 4QFlor 12-13) and applied to the Qumran group's history. Vs. 16 (Amos 9:11) speaks of the restoration of the true people of God (Acts 1—7); vs. 17 (Amos 9:12) of the inclusion of non-Jews (Acts 8— 14). The evidence of experience (i.e., what God is obviously doing) is in continuity with what Scripture says (i.e., nothing is said in Amos 9:11–12 that suggests that the Gentiles have to become Jews in order to become God's people).

(b) The evidence having been presented, James then offers a proposal in two parts (vss. 19–21). The first part consists of his judgment that on the basis of Peter's experience and the Scripture's witness "we should not trouble those of the Gentiles who turn to God" (vs. 19). The principle is established. Salvation is apart from the law. The second part of James' proposal is his suggestion that the Jerusalem body should write the Gentile Christians about what is necessary to enable conscientious Torah-keeping Jewish Christians to fellowship with them freely (vss. 20–21; that this was a problem is evidenced by Gal 2:11–21). To enable fellowship without offence to Jews and Jewish Christians, Gentile Christians need to observe four things: first, do not eat anything sacrificed to heathen gods (see Lev 17:8–9); second, abstain from incestuous marriages (see Lev 18:6–18); third, do not eat meat of strangled animals (see Lev 17:13–14); and fourth, abstain from partaking of blood (see Lev 17:10–12; Gen 9:4). In Lev 17—18 these rules apply both to Jews and to the resident aliens. The Lukan James, then, would seem to regard the Gentiles as analogous to the "strangers" of the OT (see Lev 19:33–34). If the Gentiles will follow these guidelines, then fellowship of Jews and Gentiles within the church will not be hampered. An accommodation is proposed. Let the Gentiles do the minimum necessary to enable table fellowship with conscientious Jewish Christians.

The proposal of James seems good to the church. The letter upholding the principle of a gospel free from law and the appeal for accommodation by the Gentile Christians is sent by Judas and Silas, two Jerusalem Christians, along with Barnabas and Paul to Antioch (vss. 22–29). Acknowledging that the accommodation asked is a burden, the letter says it is no more than is absolutely necessary (vs. 28).

(3) The outcome of the Council is narrated in vss. 30–35. When the messengers go down to Antioch and read the letter, the congregation there rejoices. It is an acceptable solution for all concerned. After a time the Jerusalem representatives return home, leaving Paul and Barnabas to continue their teaching and preaching of the word of the Lord.

It will be possible to recognize the functions of Acts 15 as a whole within Luke-Acts if we recognize a certain pattern in the Lukan narrative. In Acts 1:8//9:15–16 we find a commission given by the risen Lord; in Acts 10//13—14 there is a move to the Gentiles directed by the Lord; in Acts 11:1–18//15:1–21 we have a confirmation by Jerusalem of the prior mission to the Gentiles; in Acts 11:19–30; 12:25//15:22–35, especially vs. 31, there occur gestures of Christian unity on the part of the Gentile Christians. Seen in the context of this pattern, Acts 15 serves both to legitimate the law-free gospel of the Pauline mission, past and future, and to show how those victorious in matters of principle are solicitous of the feelings of the others, the end in view being Christian unity without compromise.

This passage can yield a timely sermon entitled, "When Missionaries Cause Trouble Back Home." In the twentieth century when foreign missionaries have returned home with views on race, ecumenism, and the Holy Spirit often at variance with the established bodies that sent them out, Acts 15 speaks a relevant word. In the first place, we see that on the mission field racial barriers and certain religious mores were transcended (15:12, 13–14). The Gentiles were included by virtue of their religious experience, without becoming Jews first. In the second place, what was practiced on the mission field created problems back home (15:1–5). In the third place, gains made on the mission field found support at home. This was due both to the experience of key leaders at home (15:7–11) and to Scripture seen now in a new light (15:13–18). Finally, persons connected with the mission field, where principle was not involved, tried to be sensitive to the feelings of the established church at home (15:20, 28–29, 31). Ecclesiastes says there is a time for everything. Acts 15 depicts a situation in which there is both a time to stand for principle and a time to accommodate. From Luke's perspective, only those led by the Spirit can tell the difference.

A Prerequisite for Church Growth (15:36—16:5)

Acts 15:36—21:16 (17?) is a thought unit in two parts: (1) 15:36—18:22, and (2) 18:23—21:16 (see Luke 19:45—21:38—(1) 19:47—21:4, and (2) 21:5–38). It is framed by the two passages that have Paul in Jerusalem, relating what God has done through him among the Gentiles and being affirmed by the Jerusalem Christians. These texts state the terms of the letter, and tell of Paul's actions designed to pacify Jewish sensitivities (15:1–35 and 21:17–26). The text of Acts does not indicate a clear break between what are usually called the second and third missionary journeys. The focus for part one, Acts 15:36—18:22, is Macedonia and Achaia. The surface structure is fairly simple.

A—The commission to return to visit churches previously founded (15:36–41)
  B—The visit to Galatia (16:1–5)
A′—The commission to go into Europe (16:6–10)
  B′—The visits to Philippi (16:11–40), to Thessalonica (17:1–9), to Beroea (17:10–14), to Athens (17:15–34), and to Corinth (18:1–18a)
    C—Travel summary (18:18b–22)

Of the sections narrating visits to various cities, only those dealing with Philippi, Athens, and Corinth are much more than summaries. The focus for part two, Acts 18:23—21:16, is Ephesus. Again the surface structure is a simple one.

Travel summary (18:23)
  Activities in Ephesus (18:24—19:41)
Travel summary (20:1–6)
  Activities in Troas (20:7–12)
Travel summary (20:13–16)
  Activity in Miletus (20:17–38)
Travel summary (21:1–7)
  Activity in Caesarea (21:8–14)
Travel summary (21:15–17)

Four sections, those dealing with activities in various cities, are more than summaries.

Within this larger unit, Acts 15:36—16:5 is a smaller sub-unit held together by an inclusion (15:36—return and visit churches established earlier; 16:5—so the churches were strengthened and increased). At least three major Lukan themes are found in its verses. (1) There are four major moves to the Gentiles in Acts: (a) Peter in chapter 10; (b) anonymous men of Cyprus and Cyrene in 11:19–21; (c) Paul and Barnabas in chapters 13—14; and (d) Paul and Silas in Acts 16—20. In each of these cases the extension to the Gentiles is followed by an episode of Jerusalem approval: (a) 11:1–18; (b) 11:22–24; (c) chapter 15; and (d) 21:17–25. In each of the last three, after the principle of Gentile inclusion is established, there is a gesture on the part of the Gentile Christians or missionaries of solidarity with the other side: (a) 11:27–30; (b) 15:31 (see 16:4); and (c) 21:20–24, 26. It is in this context that Acts 15:36—16:5 must first be viewed.

The church at Antioch, in response to the Jerusalem Council, acts in two ways that reflect its agreement with the Council's decisions. First, in 15:31 they agree with the terms of the decree. Second, in 15:40 they commend Paul and Silas on their new mission to the Gentiles. Paul's actions in this section reflect the same concern for both principle and accommodation. On the one hand, he lives out of the established principle. In 15:36 he revisits the brethren; in 16:6–10 he sets off on a new outreach. On the other hand, he is accommodating. He chooses Silas to be his partner (15:40), that is, a Jerusalem Christian who brought the letter to Antioch (15:22–23). He circumcises Timothy (16:3), a man well spoken of by the brethren in Galatia (16:2; see 1 Tim 3:7). Timothy was the son of a Jewish mother and a Gentile father. Under Jewish law such marriages were frowned on. If they took place, however, the offspring was regarded as Jewish. Timothy, by Jewish custom, was liable to circumcision. Since he had not been circumcised and since Paul wanted him to accompany him, Paul circumcised Timothy (16:3). This was to avoid giving any offense to the Jews with whom they would most certainly work (see 1 Cor 9:19–23 which would take precedence over 1 Cor 7:17–24). He also delivers the decree of Jerusalem (15:20, 29) not only to the churches so specified in the Jerusalem letter (15:23—Antioch, Syria, Cilicia) but also to the Galatian churches as well (16:1–2, 4). This shows the lie of the charges made against him in Acts 21:21. The first theme characteristic of Luke to be found in these verses is that once a principle is vindicated, those victorious try to accommodate the other side in areas where their feelings are sensitive.

(2) A second Lukan theme has to do with the selection of qualified leadership to enable a new task to be undertaken. In 1:15–26 Matthias was chosen to complete the Twelve who were to bear witness to Israel's twelve tribes; in 6:1–6 the Seven were chosen to remedy the injustices in the distribution to widows in the early church; in 11:25–26 Barnabas went to find Saul to enlist him in the work with the new church at Antioch. So here in 16:3 Paul chose Timothy to accompany him just before the dawning of the mission to Europe. In each case the qualifications of the ones chosen are crucial. Acts 1:21–22 requires Matthias to have been with Jesus from his baptism by John until the ascension; Acts 6:1–6 specifies that the Seven are to be full of the Spirit and of wisdom, as well as of good repute; Saul was a Hellenist himself who had been converted and so was equipped to work with Hellenistic Jews and Gentiles in Antioch. So here Paul chose Timothy who is well spoken of by the brethren in Galatia (16:2; see 2 Tim 1:5; 3:14–15) and circumcises him so he will be acceptable to law abiding Jews and Jewish Christians. In every instance when a new task demands new leadership, the emphasis is on the qualifications of the one(s) to serve.

(3) A third Lukan theme that crops up again in this passage is the conviction that nothing can stop the spread of the gospel. In Acts 5:19 the imprisoned apostles are freed from prison by an angel; in 8:1, 4 the persecution that arose after Stephen's martyrdom simply scattered the sparks of the gospel flame; in chapter 9 the great persecutor of the church, Saul, is overpowered by the risen Lord and turned into a missionary for the very cause he tried to destroy; in 12:7–11 Peter is freed from prison by an angel of the Lord in answer to the church's prayers; in 13:6–12 in a showdown with a powerful magician, the gospel is victorious. Nothing outside the church can stop the mission commanded by the risen Jesus (1:8). In 15:39–40, we learn that even dissension within the ranks of the church's missionaries cannot stifle the missionary outreach. When Paul and Barnabas quarrel over John Mark (15:37–38), the result is two mission efforts in-

stead of one. God overrides even human division within the
community to see his will accomplished. The conclusion to
which the entire thought unit moves is found in 16:5: "So the
churches were strengthened in the faith, and they increased
in numbers daily." This qualitative and quantitative growth
occurred in spite of human frailty, aided by new and qualified leadership, and spurred on by a firm commitment to
principle (a law free gospel) and a desire to accommodate the
style of mission to take account of the sensitivities of those
being dealt with.

A sermon based on this text might be entitled, "A Prerequisite for Church Growth." The concluding summary (16:5) refers to the matter of church growth. The rest of the passage
leads up to this statement. In the unit, Paul is portrayed as a
model to emulate. Paul's example in this context shows a
prerequisite for church growth to be nurture. Acts 15:36 has
Paul say: "Come, let us return and visit the brethren in every
city where we proclaimed the word of the Lord, and see how
they are." Acts 15:41 says: "And he went through Syria and
Cilicia, strengthening the churches." Acts 16:1 says: "And he
came also to Derbe and to Lystra." The Lukan Paul did not
"dip them and drop them." He was concerned to nurture
them. Paul's nurture of his churches was based on a correct
strategy. This strategy was twofold: (1) be sure about the essence of the faith and defend it (see Acts 15:3, 12—the law
free gospel); (2) be accommodating where principle is not involved (Acts 16:3, 4). Nurture based on a correct strategy
yields growth, both qualitatively (16:5—"So the churches
were strengthened in the faith") and quantitatively (16:5—
"and they increased in numbers daily"). The apostle Paul
(14:4, 14) is depicted in this text in the exemplary posture of
nurturing the churches he had founded, holding firmly to the
principle of the law free gospel but otherwise accommodating himself to the sensitivities of those with whom he
worked. This form of nurture produced church growth in maturity and yielded the fruit of further outreach. Acts 15:36—
16:5 holds up nurture as a prerequisite for church growth.

What Does the Gospel Do? (16:6–40)

Acts 16:6–40 is a thought unit in two parts: (1) vss. 6–10,
the commission to evangelize Macedonia, and (2) vss. 11–40,

the missionary work in Philippi, the leading city of the district of Macedonia. (1) In vss. 6–10 there is a major turning point in the narrative of the Christian mission in Acts. Christianity is now moving into a new area, Europe. Paul goes there as a result of divine guidance, both negative (vss. 6, 7) and positive: "And a vision appeared to Paul in the night: a man of Macedonia was standing beseeching him and saying, 'Come over to Macedonia and help us'" (vs. 9). Like Peter's move to the Gentiles in Acts 10, Paul's entry into Europe results from a vision (10:17). In both cases, the point is that the outreach is due, not to human desire, but solely to God's intervention. The direct religious experience enables the fulfillment of the command of the risen Jesus in Acts 1:8.

(2) Acts 16:11–40 is a sub-unit bracketed by references to Lydia (vss. 14, 40) and to the believers in the city of Philippi (vss. 15, 40). When Paul goes out to the place of prayer and speaks to the women gathered there (vs. 13), a rich businesswoman, Lydia, a seller of purple goods and a worshiper of God, is converted (vs. 14). Rich business people are touched by the gospel as well as slave girls (vss. 16–18) and middle class jailers (vss. 30–34). When the Evangelist says, "the Lord opened her heart to give heed to what was said by Paul" (vs.14), he is indicating that conversion is due to God's initiative. Once converted, Lydia reflects the Christian traits of being hospitable (see Rom 12:13; 1 Tim 3:2; Heb 13:2; 1 Pet 4:9; 3 John 5–8) and sharing material goods with those who teach the word (see Gal 6:6; 1 Cor 9:14). That Paul stayed in the house of a Gentile Christian indicates that Lydia was accepted as a Christian of equal standing (see 10:15, 20, 28–29, 34; 11:2). Jews had an ambivalent attitude towards proselytes and God-fearers. Despite their adoption of Judaism, social inequality between them and Jews remained a reality. The narrative of Acts implies that such social inequality as existed between Jews and God-fearers does not exist within the Christian movement.

Within the frame (vss. 14–15, 40) there is a miracle story with the predictable components: (1) the ailment (vss. 16–18a)—a slave girl has a spirit of divination; (2) the cure (vs. 18b)—exorcism (see Luke 4:18; 8:26–39, Jesus' universal authority over evil powers is foreshadowed); (3) the reaction to the cure (vss. 19–24). The third component of the miracle

story has been expanded drastically (see 14:11–18) in order
to perform various other functions within the narrative.

(a) When the slave girl's owners see that their hope of gain
is gone, they seize Paul and Silas and drag them into the
marketplace before the rulers (vs. 19). It is a Lukan belief
that vested financial interests, when threatened, oppose the
gospel. This fact of life was foreshadowed in Luke 8:37 where
the Gerasenes ask Jesus to leave their country because the
healing of the demoniac cost them financially. This emphasis
will crop up again in Acts 19:23–41 when, in Ephesus, the
business of those who make silver shrines of Artemis is
threatened by the gospel. The economic motivation of those
opposed to the Christian missionaries is masked behind various other appeals: Paul and Silas are branded as foreigners
(an appeal to nationalistic feeling); they are labeled Jews (an
appeal to racial prejudice); they are described as purveyors
of new ideas (an appeal to traditionalism); and they are depicted as opposed to Rome (an appeal to patriotism).

(b) Vss. 22–34 tell of the combination of mob violence, official beating, and imprisonment that result from the machi-
nations of the vested economic interests in Philippi. These
verses also say that nothing, including state action, can stop
God's advance: "and suddenly there was a great earthquake
(see 4:31), so that the foundations of the prison were shaken;
and immediately all the doors were opened and everyone's
fetters were unfastened" (vs. 26; see 5:17–21; 12:1–19). Aware
of this victorious thrust of the gospel, the two imprisoned
missionaries pray and sing hymns to God. Here is depicted
Christian fearlessness in the face of unjust and threatening
pagan actions (see Phil 1:28–30; 1 Pet 3:14b). As a result of
the miracle of the freeing of the prisoners, the jailer could
believe what the spirit of divination said ("These men are
servants of the Most High God, who proclaim to you the way
of salvation"—vs. 17; Luke 4:41; 8:28) was true. The miracle
in the jail is not so much for the security of Paul and Silas as
for the salvation of the jailer (see Acts 9:35, 42). He, therefore,
beseeches them: "Men, what must I do to be saved?" (vs. 30).
The answer he receives is the traditional Christian answer:
"Believe in the Lord Jesus, and you will be saved" (vs. 31; see
Rom 10:9; 1 Cor 12:3; Phil 2:11). As in the case of Lydia, his
conversion is followed by baptism and by acts of hospitality

in which he shares his material goods with Paul and Silas (see Acts 2:44–46; 4:32–35; 11:27–30; 16:15). The jailer's actions, moreover, depict the traditional Christian trait of compassion for prisoners (see Heb 10:34; 13:3; Matt 25:36; Lucian, *Peregrinus*, 12–13). Just as in the case of the great persecutor, Saul, in Acts 9, the jailer here in Philippi gives immediate evidence of the genuineness of his conversion.

(c) In vss. 35–40 we hear that the magistrates feel that beating and imprisonment have surely taught the outsiders their lesson, so they order Paul and Silas released. The jailer is thrilled for his new found Christian brethren and bids them, "Go in peace" (vs. 36). Paul, however, is unwilling for the matter to end there. "They have beaten us publicly (see 2 Cor 11:25), uncondemned men who are Roman citizens (see Acts 22:25), and have thrown us into prison; and do they now cast us out secretly? No. Let them come themselves and take us out" (vs. 37). This brings fear to the officials who have acted out of line. They, therefore, come and apologize for their mistakes. This paragraph makes three points for Luke's readers about the Christians' relation to the State. First, it shows the legitimacy of Christians' appealing to their legal rights as protection against unjust treatment by non-Christians (see 22:25; 25:11). Second, it claims that the State is reasonable and will correct its mistakes when these are made clear. Roman justice is basically reliable. Third, it makes very clear that Christians are not trouble makers but are victims of those with questionable motives. This is seen in the vindication of the mistreated missionaries. This paragraph also reiterates a point made earlier in 15:36—16:5 about Paul. This missionary is concerned not only about converting people but also about nurturing them. So after the official apology, before leaving the city, Paul and Silas "visited Lydia; and when they had seen the brethren, they exhorted them" (vs. 40). Only then does Paul depart.

This passage, Acts 16:6–40, can be preached in a number of ways. One sermon seed is found in vss. 6–10. When God closes doors, it is because he had another for us to pass through. If one starts reading the passage in this way, then vss. 11–40 say: the door that is right to pass through does not guarantee the comfort of the Christian but the success of the mission.

✝ Another sermon seed, perhaps for Labor Day, derives from the Lukan emphasis on the opposition between the gospel and the "demonic-economic-political complex" (i.e., profit based on human exploitation). The words of Halford E. Luccock, *The Acts of the Apostles in Present-Day Preaching* (Chicago: Willett, Clark & Co., 1942), p. 145, are suggestive: "If profit-makers shout at a vigorous Christianity, 'You are hurting my business,' let the church maintain: '*You* are hurting *my* business. My business is the welfare of the sons and daughters of Almighty God.' "

Yet another sermon that captures the essence of the text picks up on the focus on the preaching of the gospel (16:10— "preach the gospel"; 16:17—"proclaim to you the way of salvation"; 16:31—"Believe on the Lord Jesus"). According to 16:10, vss. 11–40 tell of the preaching of the gospel in Philippi. "What Does the Gospel Do?" Acts 16:6–40 says it does two things. In the first place, the gospel presses toward a universal outreach. On the one hand, there is a geographical universalism (see 16:9–10); on the other, there is a social universalism that encompasses the rich (16:14–15; see Luke 19:1–10), the poor (16:16–18; see Luke 4:18), and the middle class (16:30–34; see Luke 5:1–11). In the second place, the gospel produces certain fruits in those who respond positively. There is private confession, Jesus is Lord (16:31), enabled by God (16:14; see 1 Cor 12:3). There is public declaration, baptism (16:15, 33). There are personal demonstrations, kindness (16:33a) and generosity (16:15, 34), which put economic resources in the service of faith in contrast to the demonic-economic stance which used wealth solely for private gain (16:16, 19). Viewed in this way, Acts 16 becomes a narrative picture of what the gospel does.

Radical Monotheism and Modern Idolatry
(17:15–34)

Following the divine commission to go into Europe (16:6–10), Paul visits Philippi (16:11–40), Thessalonica (17:1–9), Beroea (17:10–14), and now Athens (17:15–34). Next he will go to Corinth (18:1–18). Only the sections narrating the visits to Philippi, Athens, and Corinth are more than summaries. Acts 17:15–34 tells of Paul's stay in the university city of Athens. It begins in 17:15 with his coming to the

city; it ends in 18:1a with his leaving Athens. This section
falls into three parts: (1) the context (vss. 16–21); (2) the sermon (vss. 22–31); and (3) the conclusion (vss. 32–34).

(1) In the first of these parts, vss. 16–21, the reader learns
the intent of the section. It will be an attack on pagan idolatry. (a) The usual Lukan pattern for Paul's missionary work
in Acts is to have him go into the synagogue and argue with
the Jews and God-fearers (e.g., 13:5, 14, 43; 14:1; 16:13; 17:1,
10, 17; 18:4, 19; 19:8). This is also found here (17:17—"so he
argued in the synagogue with the Jews and the devout persons"). By the inclusion of vs. 16, however, Luke changes the
direction of the readers' attention: "Now while Paul was
waiting for them at Athens, his spirit was provoked within
him as he saw the city was full of idols." A university city like
Athens blends enlightened philosophy and superstitious idolatry. Learning does not eliminate idolatry. The Lukan Paul is
not so much impressed by Athens' culture as he is irritated
by its idolatry. This is the springboard from which the passage moves.

(b) Paul's observation of Athenian idolatry (vs. 16) is given
concrete form in vs. 18. Some of the Epicurean and Stoic philosophers he meets suppose Paul to be talking about two new
deities to add to their pantheon when he preaches Jesus (a
masculine word in Greek) and the Anastasis or resurrection
(a feminine term in Greek). Their very way of hearing expos-
es their polytheistic presuppositions. They identify Paul with
the many advocates of the Eastern cults now spilling over
into the West. These philosophers bring him to the Areopagus, probably the Athenian court which met in the Stoa
Basileios in the Agora and which still exercized authority in
matters of religion and education. Unlike Socrates who had
stood trial for teaching new divinities, Paul is brought merely to satisfy the insatiable curiosity of the Athenians and the
foreigners living there (vs. 21). Athenians were well known
for their curiosity (see Demosthenes, *Oration*, 4:10). The Pauline intent is different. Here before the intelligensia of the
most learned city in the world, Paul gives a Christian critique of pagan idolatry.

(2) The speech itself comes in vss. 22–31. Its introduction
(vss. 22–23) is masterful. As ancient rhetoric dictated, Paul
tries to win over his audience in the beginning. First, rather

than display his irritation at their idolatry (vs. 16), Paul praises the Athenians: "Men of Athens, I perceive that in every way you are very religious. For as I passed along, and observed the objects of your worship, I found also an altar with this inscription, 'To an unknown god.' " (Pausanias, about A.D. 150 says that near Athens were "altars of gods both named and unknown." Philostratus, *Life of Apollonius of Tyana*, 6:3:5, has his hero say that in Athens there were altars of unknown gods erected. No such inscription has yet been found.) Paul then declares that, contrary to the philosophers' charge (vs. 19–20) and unlike Socrates, he is not teaching anything new or strange. "What therefore you worship as unknown, this I proclaim to you" (vs. 23b). Paul's inference is that his hearers have both a positive and a negative relation with his God. They worship him (so the altar) but do not know him (hence the inscription). What he proposes to do is not to tell them about a new deity but to acquaint them with the one already honored but not understood.

After the ingratiating introduction, the bulk of the speech (vss. 24–31) is an elaboration of the Hellenistic Christian kerygma echoed in 1 Thess 1:9–10: (a) "you turned to God from idols, to serve a living and true God"—first, an affirmation of monotheism; and (b) "to wait for his Son from heaven, whom he raised from the dead, Jesus who delivers us from the wrath to come"—second, a proclamation of the risen Christ as cosmic judge. (a) The affirmation of monotheism is found in vss. 24–30. This unknown god whom you worship is the self-sufficient (vs. 25—see 2 Macc 14:35), cosmic (vs. 24b—see Acts 7:48–49) Creator (vs. 24a—see Acts 14:15) who made the world and all peoples who live in it (vs. 26—see Isa 42:5). This God made us so that we might seek him and hopefully find him (vss. 27–28—see Eusebius, *Preparation for the Gospel*, 13:12:3ff., where the Hellenistic Jew Aristobulus had already taken over the quotaton from Aratus in vs. 28 and interpreted it in Jewish terms as part of Jewish apologetic against pagan idolatry). Given these facts, all attempts to reduce God to something he has made are folly (vs. 29). Up until now God has overlooked our ignorance (vs. 30a—see Acts 14:16), but now he "commands all men everywhere to repent" (vs. 30b). Repentance here means turning from our ignorance (i.e., our worshiping something God made rather than the God who made it) and turning to the living God, the Creator (see Ps 115:4–8; Wisdom of Solomon 13:10; 14:8–12; 15:7–17).

(b) The proclamation of the risen Christ as cosmic judge comes only at the very end of the speech (vs. 31—see 3:19–21; Luke 21:27, 34–36; 12:40). God the Creator has fixed a day of universal judgment and has appointed as judge the man whom he has raised from the dead (see Aeschylus, *Eumenides*, 647ff., who has the god Apollo deny the resurrection on the occasion of the inauguration of the court of the Areopagus). The Evangelist has the Lukan Paul say that God's attitude has changed. Before the resurrection of Jesus, he overlooked human ignorance. Since then, he demands repentance. In this context, therefore, for Paul to preach Jesus and the resurrection (vs. 18b) is for him to proclaim God's universal judgment of idolatry (vs. 31).

(3) The conclusion (vss. 32–34) reflects the same division in the responses to the gospel that have been met elsewhere (13:43, 45, 48; 14:4, 17:4–5, 12–13). It is instructive to note the extremes of those who respond positively: a member of the court (Dionysius the Areopagite) and probably a courtesan (a woman named Damaris). The Christian gospel is the exclusive property neither of an oligarchy nor of the proletariat, though members of both are drawn into it (see Luke 16:16). When some say, "We will hear you again about this" (vs. 32), their response foreshadows that of Felix in Acts 24:25.

Acts 17:15–34 is a Christian critique of idolatry. As such its message is relevant to today. A sermon on this passage might be entitled, "Radical Monotheism and Modern Idolatry." The introduction would orient the hearers to the story of Paul in Athens and focus their attention on its intent, a Christian critique of idolatry. The text first of all states the problem, idolatry. On the one side, there is the matter of what it is. Idolatry is the opposite of true worship. It is the worship of something or someone God has made rather than the Creator who made it or him/her. It is giving a relative good an absolute value and thereby perverting it. On the other side, there is the matter of whom it infects. Idolatry infects the learned as well as the sensual. Learning does not eliminate idolatry. It just makes it more sophisticated. The text secondly speaks about the prospect for idolaters, judgment. The Creator will hold a cosmic trial. The time has been set ("he has fixed a day on which he will judge the world"), so it is certain. The judge has been chosen: "he will judge the world in righteousness by a man whom he has appointed" (Acts 10:42). It is the one who was faithful unto death (Luke 22:39–46). The notice has been posted: "And of this he has given assurance to all men by raising him from the dead." Given the human problem (idolatry) and the divine prospect (judgment), we, like the Athenians, are called upon to repent: turn from, turn to.

Roots and New Shoots in Religion (18:1–22)

Acts 18:1–18a, the account of Paul's stay in Corinth begins with his going there (vs. 1b) and ends with his taking leave (vs. 18b). References to Aquila and Priscilla frame the narrative (vss. 2, 18c), just as the story of Paul's visit to Philippi was framed by references to Lydia (16:14, 40). The statement about Paul's working with them as a tentmaker (18:3, see 1 Thess 2:9; 2 Thess 3:7–8) anticipates his later farewell speech in which he says: "You yourselves know that these hands ministered to my necessities" (20:34). This combination of teaching and working at a trade was a Jewish ideal (see *Pirke Aboth*, 2:2). That vs. 18d refers to a vow Paul makes (see Num 6:1–21; 1 Macc 3:49; Acts 21:23–26) gives the Corinth episode yet another frame, that of Paul the faithful Jew.

Within the frame the narrative falls into a clearcut pattern.

A—Paul's full time preaching (vs. 5) in response to the arrival of Silas and Timothy
  B—By-products of the preaching
    1. Jewish opposition in the synagogue (vss. 5b–6a)
    2. Pauline responses, nonverbal (vs. 6a) and verbal (vs. 6b)
    3. Remedy for the situation (vs. 7)
    4. Good results (vs. 8)
A'—Paul's long term teaching (vs. 11) in response to the vision (vs. 9)
  B'—By-products of the teaching
    1. Jewish opposition in court (vss. 12–13)
    2. Pauline response unnecessary (vs. 14a)
    3. Remedy for the situation (vss. 14b–17)
    4. Good results (vs. 18a)

This pattern is a variant of that used for Paul's earlier visit to Antioch of Pisidia (13:14–52).

A—Paul preaches (16b–41, 44) in response to the invitation of the rulers of the synagogue (vs. 15) and to the people's request (vs. 42)
    B—By-products of the preaching
      1. Jewish opposition in the synagogue (vs. 45)
      2. Pauline response (vss. 46–47)
      3. Good results (vs. 48)
A'—The word of the Lord spread (vs. 49)
    B'—By-products
      1. Jewish opposition (vs. 50)
      2. Pauline response (vs. 51)
      3. Good results (vs. 52)

What is missing in Acts 13 are two things: (1) the component that gives the remedy for the situation, and (2) the prophecy-fulfillment schema of vss. 9–10, 11–17. Any discussion of the passage in Acts 18 will need to follow the pattern and focus on the distinctives.

When Paul comes to Corinth (vs. 1), he finds the Jewish Christians, Aquila and Priscilla (vs. 2; 1 Cor 16:19; Rom 16:3–4; 2 Tim 4:19), victims of Claudius' expulsion of the Jews from Rome about A.D. 49. (Suetonius' "Life of Claudius," 25:4, says: "Since the Jews were continually making disturbances at the instigation of Chrestus, he [Claudius] expelled them from Rome.") Paul stayed and worked with them since they were also tentmakers (vs. 3). This work left him only the sabbath to preach in the synagogue (vs. 4). As the result of the coming of Silas and Timothy from Macedonia, presumably with a gift (2 Cor 11:9; Phil 4:15), Paul now devotes himself entirely to preaching (vs. 5—the RSV misses the point that the NEB and NIV catch).

Paul's preaching that the Christ is Jesus evokes Jewish opposition (vss. 5b–6a). He then responds nonverbally ("he shook out his garments"—see Neh 5:13) and verbally ("Your blood be upon your heads: I am innocent. From now on I will go to the Gentiles"—vs. 6). The remedy that Luke proposes for Paul's separation from the synagogue is to have him move to "the house of a man named Titius Justus," a Gentile God-fearer who lived next door to the synagogue (vs. 7—foreshadowing 19:8–9). The results of this preaching in the new place are good: "Crispus, the ruler of the synagogue, believed in the Lord," as well as many others (vs. 8).

Vss. 9–17 constitute a prophecy-fulfillment schema: (1) the prophecy is in two parts (vss. 9–10)—(a) "speak and do not be silent" (vs. 9), and (b) "no man shall attack you to harm you" (vs. 10); and (2) the fulfillment is in two parts—(a) "And he stayed a year and six months, teaching the word of God" (vs. 11); and (b) the Gallio episode (vss. 12–17). When the Jews bring Paul before Gallio, they say: "This man is persuading men to worship God contrary to the law" (vs. 13). A Pauline response is rendered unnecessary by Gallio's remedy. He takes "law" to mean Jewish law rather than Roman law (as in 16:21), concluding that Paul's conduct does not fall into the category of crimes against the State. He drives the Jews from the tribunal, saying: "I refuse to be a judge of these things" (vs. 15). Then, either an anti-Semitic crowd beats the ruler of the synagogue or the Jews do so, perhaps because he had Christian sympathies (vs. 17). However it is interpreted, Gallio pays no attention. Unlike Antioch where Paul had been driven out of the Jewish district (13:50), in Corinth Paul stays "many days longer" (18:18a). When he leaves (vs. 18b), it is not under compulsion but freely.

Literarily, this prophecy-fulfillment schema functions to set the stage for what follows. At the end of Acts the narrative flow is controlled even more than before by the prophecy-fulfillment pattern (see 21:11; 23:11; 27:24). The occurrence of so obvious an instance of fulfillment here following closely on the heels of the prophecy alerts the hearers to what will follow and gives them confidence that what is prophesied later will have its fulfillment. This is akin to Luke 22:10–12 (prophecy) and 13 (fulfillment) which both prepares for Jesus' prophecies to follow and instills confidence in their fulfillment (22:14–38; 22:69; 23:29–31; 23:43; 24:49; Acts 1:8).

Theologically, different parts of the Corinth episode function to say several things. (1) Work is a part of the Christian lifestyle (see 1 Thess 2:9; 4:11–12; 2 Thess 3:6–13; Mark 6:3). (2) The prophecy fulfillment schema serves the same function here that the deliverance from prison served in Acts 5; 12; 16.

It shows the providential care of his servants exercised by the Lord. (3) The positive picture of Gallio here fits into another major Lukan theme. The State generally is regarded as a protection against Jewish and pagan hatred (cf. 19:23–41; 21:31–36; 23:12–35). It does not regard Christianity as such as criminal. (4) When Luke inverts the order of the names of Aquila and Priscilla (vs. 2) to Priscilla and Aquila (vss. 18, 26), it is as significant as the earlier inversion of Barnabas and Saul (13:2, 7) to Paul and his company (13:13) or Paul and Barnabas (13:43, 46, 50). To put one's name first seems to be the Evangelist's way of indicating who has the leadership role. If so, then this detail fits into the general Lukan emphasis on women and their ministries (see Luke 8:1–3; 10:38–42; 23:49, 55–56; 24:1–11, 22–23; Acts 1:14; 9:36–43; 12:12–17, 16:14–15; 17:4, 12, 34, etc.). (5) Vss. 20–21 have Paul say to the Ephesians: "I will return to you if God wills." This legitimates the next leg of Paul's missionary travels (18:23—21:14) which is focused on Ephesus. Again, it is the author's intent to say that each part of the missionary outreach is according to the divine plan (cf. 8:26; 11:17, 13:2; 15:14–18; 16:6–10).

Taken as a whole, Acts 18:1–22 functions theologically as part of the Lukan emphasis on Christianity as a way or sect within Judaism and heir to the prophecies of the Scriptures. First, the people associated with Paul are Christian Jews who are faithful to Judaism (Aquila and Priscilla; Silas; Timothy). Second, Paul's own practices are true to Jewish ideals and mores (note his work at a trade while serving as a teacher; the vow). Third, the perception of certain key people is that Christianity is a part of Judiasm (Gallio) or the fulfillment of Judaism (Crispus). That Christianity is institutionally separate from the synagogue is due to the rejection of the latter. When Paul says "from now on I will go to the Gentiles," he does not mean that Jews are no longer to be converted (see vs. 8) any more than he means that in the future in other cities he will not go to the synagogue first (see vs. 19). What Paul must mean here is that he is now moving his "site of preaching" "in this city" from the synagogue to a Gentile house (see 11:3, 12; 13:14, 46; 16:15, 34). This gives the Christian mission the appearance of being institutionally separate from Judaism. It is Luke's intent to say that this is not true (see 21:20–25); 23:1–10; 24:10–21; 25:8; 25:18–19; 26:2–23; 28:17–20; 28:21–22). Why the strong emphasis on Christianity's being a part of Judaism? Very likely it is part of the Lukan appeal to antiquity. In Mediterranean culture, peoples often appealed to the antiquity of their community as a way of legitimating themselves or of gaining status. Such an appeal to their ancient roots would give the Christians of Luke's time a status they would not otherwise have (see, my book, *Reading Luke*, pp. 239–40).

A sermon that tries to be faithful to the thrust of the passage as a whole might be entitled "Roots and New Shoots in Religion." Such a sermon would have to explain the Lukan motif that ties Christianity to Judaism and its meaning. Then it would have to raise the question of its relevance for us. It speaks first of all about the importance of religious roots (see Luke 8:13) in the soil of Scripture and the history of God's people. It speaks also of the inevitability of new shoots within religious movements. It speaks furthermore of the imperative of recognizing the new shoots that grow out of the old roots. Some see (e.g., the missionaries, a leader of the synagogue, and the state officials), others do not (e.g., an institution with vested interests fails to see out of jealousy—13:45; 17:5). When an institution cannot see the continuity between the new shoots and the old roots, there is a problem. If God cannot work through a religious institution, he will work around it. A similar point is made about leaders of religious institutions in Luke 20:9–19 (see Luke 8:18; 11:34–36). While roots are crucial for any religious movement, new shoots will continually appear. The necessity is to be able to distinguish what shoots come out of the old roots and which do not. On this discernment hangs a religious institution's usefulness to the living God.

A Prescription for Spiritual Growth (18:23—20:1)

Acts 18:23—20:1 is the first thought unit in the larger section, 18:23—21:16, which in turn is the second half of the missionary narrative of Acts 15:36—21:16. The unity of 18:23—20:1 comes from its geographical locale, Ephesus. The general pattern of Paul's activity in Ephesus is similar to that of Corinth (18.1–18). (a) Paul goes to the synagogue to preach (18:4 // 19:8); (b) he withdraws from the synagogue and teaches elsewhere with good results (18:6–8 // 19:9–10); (c) an attack is made on Paul but government officials protect him (18:12–17 // 19:23–41). The Ephesian narrative contains some distinctive variations on the pattern as well. (a) There are two episodes that refer to John's baptism (18:24–28; 19:1–7) that precede the pattern. (b) There are two units that clarify the nature of spiritual power in Christianity and in magic (19:11–12; 19:13–20). (c) There is the initiation of the motif of Paul's going to Jerusalem (19:21–22). (c) The attack made on Paul is not from the Jews but from the businessmen who profit from the cult of Artemis (19:23–41). Each of these components needs examination.

(1) In 18:24–28 and 19:1–7 one finds two stories situated in Ephesus (18:24; 19:1), referring to John's baptism (18:25; 19:3), in which those knowing or having experienced John's baptism have their knowledge (18:26) or experience (19:4–6) completed by the associates of Paul (18:26) or by Paul himself (19:6). These links show clearly that the author of Acts intended these two stories to be read together and to be understood in terms of the Pauline gospel's completion of those deficient in either doctrine or experience. In each case, note that those deficient in some way regard themselves as disciples (18:25; 19:1). In each case, their deficiency is said to be the limitation of knowledge (18:25) or experience (19:2–3) to the baptism of John. That is, either in doctrine or in experience they had an under-realized eschatology, one deficient in its understanding and experience of the Holy Spirit. In 18:24–28 a woman teacher instructs a male preacher, showing that in the post-Pauline period 1 Tim 2:12 was not regarded as a guideline for all circumstances. In 19:6, the gift of the Holy Spirit is not tied to baptism but is linked to the post-baptismal laying on of Paul's hands (see 8:14–17), indicating that for Luke the experience of the Spirit cannot be confined to sacramental impartation (Luke 3:21–22; Acts 10:44; 11:15).

(2) In 19:11–20 there are two units: (a) vss. 11–12 which tell of the miracles done by God through Paul (see Acts 5:15; Luke 6:19; 8:43–48), and (b) vss. 13–20 which describe an abortive attempt to use the name of Jesus by some Jewish

exorcists and the effects this had on many believers. In the
first unit, the miraculous power of God to heal is, as in the
case of Jesus and Peter, linked in some way to Paul's body
and clothing. Since this has, on first glance in antiquity as
well as in modern times, a magical cast to it, it is followed by
a story about Jewish magicians (see Luke 11:19; Josephus,
Antiquities, 8:2:5). Since a magician has no personal relationship with the power involved but simply uses it for his own
purposes, these exorcists who are non-Christians attempt to
use the name of Jesus with whom Paul has the relationship
(vs. 13). They fail, as Luke narrates humorously, with the result that many Christians confess their own involvement
with magic and renounce it at real cost to themselves (vs.
19). The Lukan point is that the spiritual power manifest
through Christians like Paul is not appropriated or dispensed
as a commodity (see Acts 8:18–23), but is the result of a personal relationship with the heavenly Lord. Recognition of
this fact leads to the renunciation of magical practices by
Christians. Justin Martyr (*I Apology*, 14) states the Christian
posture: "we who formerly used magical arts, dedicate ourselves to the good and unbegotten God." That Christian attitudes towards spiritual power need refinement and
purification tells the reader that Christians are not totally
converted when they first become disciples.

(3) In 19:21–22 there is a foreshadowing of the remainder
of Paul's ministry in Acts. He resolves in the Spirit "to pass
through Macedonia and Achaia (see 20:1–12) and to go to Jerusalem" (see 21:15–38) and then to Rome (see 28:14–16).
Two emphases stand out here. On the one hand, the resolve
to pass through Macedonia and Achaia is connected with
Paul's work of strengthening the disciples made on earlier
trips (see 18:23; 20:2). As elsewhere (15:36, 41), the Lukan
Paul not only evangelizes but also nurtures. In fact, 18:23,
19:21–22, 20:1–2, give this section a focus on spiritual
growth. Like Jesus in Luke 9:52, Paul sends his helpers on
before him in a team effort. On the other hand, the Pauline
resolve to go to Jerusalem echoes Luke 9:51 where Jesus set
his face to go to the Holy City. This is the beginning of an
extensive series of parallels between the career of Paul in
Acts and that of Jesus in Luke (see my *Reading Luke*, pp.
186–87). The Lukan Paul is thereby shown to be following

Jesus' way not only in manifesting the power of the Holy Spirit but also in passing through many tribulations on the way to the Kingdom of God (Acts 14:22; Luke 9:23; 14:27; 23:26). In this way the Evangelist avoids any temptation to an over-realized eschatology (see Luke 17:22–37).

(4) In 19:23–41 Paul, the preacher of monotheism (19:26; see 14:15–17; 17:16, 29; 1 Thess 1:9–10), evokes mob action from the devotees of Artemis of the Ephesians (see *Acts of John* 3, 37, 39, 42, 43, 46). The temple of Artemis was the foremost of the Ionian temples of the time (Pausanias 7:5:4), one of the seven wonders of the ancient world (so the epigramist Antipater). It was a central pillar in the banking structures of Asia (Dio Chrysostom, *Oration*, 31:54), as well as an asylum offering protection and relief to debtors and the helpless (Pausanias 7:2:7; Achilles Tatius, *Leucippe and Clitophon*, 7:13). The goddess and her devotees had a worldwide aspiration for the cult (Pausanias 4:31:8; Strabo 4:1:4–8; 3:4:6; Xenophon, *Anabasis*, 5:3:4–13). Luke portrays the trouble as arising out of the threat which Christian monotheism posed to the business vested interests tied up with the pagan cult (19:26–27; see 16:19; Luke 8:37). Demetrius, the silversmith, appealed to both economic and religious reasons for his opposition to Paul and his party. The Jews, through their spokesman Alexander (19:33; see 2 Tim 4:14?), try to disassociate themselves from the accused Christians to no avail (vs. 34). The town clerk then defends Paul and the Christians against the mob action. He says that the Christians are guilty neither of sacrilege (19:37) nor of criminal action (19:38, 40). The enlightened State is here portrayed as the protector of the Christians against violence stemming from the vested economic interests hiding behind religious devotion. The Asiarchs, highly respected men from the first families of the country, are sympathetic with the Christians and intervene on Paul's behalf (vs. 31; see 17:12; 17:4; 16:14; 13:7, for Luke's interest in the social standing of Christian converts or sympathizers). Christians are not the ones who disturb the public order. It is the Roman order, moreover, that is their best defense against the dangers of hostile mobs.

Acts 18:23—20:1 has two focal points, 19:23–41 being one. This section about the riot could be used in a sermon dealing with the issue of seeing religion as legitimate only when it

supports vested economic interests and as something danger-
ous when it threatens those interests. Does the economic order determine the legitimacy or illegitimacy of religion?

The other focal point yields a sermon, "A Prescription for
Spiritual Growth." The passage, with the exception of
19:23–41, has an emphasis on "strengthening disciples"
(18:23; compare 18:27; 19:21 with 20:1–2). Christians are not
born full grown. In order for them to reach maturity, there
are certain needs that must be met. On the one hand, there is
the need for the completion of those deficient in either doctrine (18:24–28) or experience (19:1–7). On the other hand,
there is the need for the correction of those not having a
proper understanding of spiritual power. Properly understood, spiritual power is not appropriated or dispensed as a
commodity but is a by-product of an intimate personal relation with the living Lord (see Acts 2:33; Luke 11:13; Phil
2:6–11; Rev 5:5). A proper understanding of spiritual power
leads to a renunciation of magical (spiritually exploitive)
practices (19:18–19). For the Third Evangelist, a growing
Christian is both one whose experience of God is not under-
realized but expanding and one whose understanding of that
relationship is being refined and purified of its deficiencies.

The Passing of the Mantle (20:17–38)

Acts 19:21 began the focus on Paul's movement to Jerusalem;
20:16 intensifies it. "Paul had decided to sail past Ephesus, so
that he would not have to spend time in Asia; for he was has-
tening to be at Jerusalem, if possible, on the day of Pentecost."
This concern of Paul, Luke says, is why the Ephesian elders
were called to meet him at Miletus (vs. 17). Between the notice
of their coming (vss. 17–18) and Paul's leaving (vss. 36–38),
there is a lengthy farewell speech of Paul (vss. 18b–35).

A farewell speech form was frequently used in ancient Judaism (e.g., Gen 49; Deut; Josh 24; 1 Sam 12; Tobit 14; *Testaments of the Twelve Patriarchs*) and in early Christianity for
Jesus (Mark 13; John 13—17; Luke 22:14–38) and for apostles
(2 Tim; 2 Pet). In Acts 20 one meets a farewell speech put into
the mouth of Paul. Farewell speeches are alike in that the hero knows he is about to die, so he calls his primary community to him and gives them a speech that includes both a
prediction of what will happen after his death and an exhor-

tation of how his hearers are to behave after his departure. The basis for the exhortation in farewell speeches of apostles is what they taught and how they behaved.

The surface structure of Acts 20:18–35 falls into three main parts: (1) vss. 18b–27; (2) vss. 28–31a; and (3) vss. 31b–35. Each of these parts needs investigation.

(1) Vss 18b–27 constitute an apology and an announcement in an ABB'A' pattern.

> A—Paul's past: apology (vss. 18b–21), using both example (vss. 18–19) and preaching (vss. 20–21; see 1 Sam 12)
> > B—Paul's future: announcement of his sufferings (vss. 22–24), beginning with "And now, behold"
> > B'—Paul's future: announcement of his death (vs. 25), beginning with "And now, behold"
> A'—Paul's past: apology (vss. 26–27), using his preaching

In this section the reader learns of the coming departure of Paul (vss. 22–24, 25) and is told that the Ephesian elders are fully instructed by Paul (vss. 20, 27).

(2) Vss. 28–31 are composed of exhortations and a prediction in an ABA' pattern.

> A—Exhortation (vs. 28) to the elders about their care of the church
> > B—Prediction (vss. 29–30) that heretics will arise
> A'—Exhortation (vs. 31) to the elders about being alert to the danger

Here is the heart of the farewell speech. The reader learns that heresy will arise after Paul's departure (see 1 Tim 1:3; 2 Tim 1:5; Rev 2:1–7, for evidence of heresy in Ephesus at the end of the first century; see Hegesippus in Eusebius, *Church History*, 3:32:7–8, for the view that heresy arose after the apostolic age) and hears Paul exhort the church officials to guard the church against this error.

(3) Vss. 31b–35 give the bases for the exhortation in vs. 31a, "Therefore be alert," in an ABA' pattern.

> A—Paul's past teaching (vs. 31b)
> > B—Paul's present blessing (vs. 32)
> A'—Paul's past example (vss. 33–35)

Here the fact that Paul taught them unstintingly and that his ministry was not subverted by love of money is a model for the Ephesian elders. His blessing commends them into God's hands. He will supply their continuing needs.

It is helpful to note that the speech has two foci: the Ephesian elders and Paul. On the one hand, it sets out certain expectations for the Christians leaders who will serve after Paul is gone from the scene. (1) They are to feed the church of the Lord (vs. 28). (2) They are to be alert to the dangers threatening the church (vss. 29–31). (3) They are not to be greedy for gain (vss. 33–35). On the other hand, the speech uses Paul as an *exempla*. (1) Paul says three times that he instructed them fully. "I did not shrink from declaring to you anything that was profitable" (vs. 20). "I did not shrink from declaring to you the whole counsel of God" (vs. 27). "For three years I did not cease night and day to admonish every one with tears" (vs. 31). What he says of his behavior in Ephesus is foreshadowed in Acts 20:7–12. In Troas Paul teaches all night, at such length that the lad Eutychus falls asleep, is killed by his fall, and must be resuscitated by the preacher. (2) The farewell speech as a whole represents Paul's alertness to the dangers to come (vss. 29–30). (3) Paul says that he "coveted no one's silver or gold or apparel" (vs. 33), and "these hands ministered to my necessities, and to those who were with me" (vs. 34). This is foreshadowed in Acts 18:3 where the narrative says Paul worked as a tentmaker with Aquila and Priscilla. So what the speech does is to set up Paul as the model for the three things the Ephesian elders are called upon to do.

Behind this surface argument are two other dimensions of Lukan thought. In the first place, the Third Evangelist roots what the church does and says in Acts in the career of the earthly Jesus. This passage is no exception. (1) The Lukan Jesus says that church leaders must be alert (Luke 12:35–40). (2) He also says they must give the household their food at the proper time (Luke 12:41–48). (3) In the speech itself, Jesus is quoted as saying: "It is more blessed to give than to receive" (vs. 35b). When this level of the Lukan argument is perceived, one can recognize that the Lukan Paul has been faithful to the words of Jesus.

In the second place, the things called for in the behavior of the Ephesian elders are a part of the general paraenesis of

the time of Luke-Acts, especially in the Pauline Circle represented by the Pastoral epistles. (1) The Pastoral epistles as a
whole reflect the need to be alert to the emergence of error in
the church in the province of Asia. (2) The leaders are called
upon to feed the church (1 Tim 3:2; 4:13–14, 16; 2 Tim 4:2;
Tit 1:9). (3) The church leaders must avoid greed (1 Tim 3:3;
Tit 1:7, 11). These parallels show that the farewell speech in
Acts 20 reflects the general concern at the end of the first century that church leaders do their jobs properly and with in-
tegrity. This concern is expressed in terms of the changing of
the guard. The older generation is departing, the mantle of
leadership is passing to the younger generation, and the new
leadership is charged to be as faithful as its predecessors.

A sermon based on this passage would function well in an
ordination service or in a seminary graduation exercise. It
might be called, "The Passing of the Mantle." The introduction would orient the hearers. This is a farewell speech. In
such speeches the object is to influence the behavior of those
addressed (portrayed as the next generation) by an appeal to
the example and teaching of the speaker (portrayed as the
generation now passing away): that is, the younger generation is asked to pick up where the older generation leaves off.
In this particular farewell speech, the speaker is Paul and the
hearers are the elders of the Ephesian church. It is concerned
to verbalize expectations for church leaders on whom the
mantle of ministry will now rest by one who has faithfully
fulfilled his commission and has obeyed the words of his
Lord. The speech is first of all an expression of concern about
the next generation's behavior. Why does the speech show
this concern? The old adage, "We are only one generation
away from barbarism," has its religious equivalent. "We are
only a generation away from a loss of faith." The new generation is faced with new challenges (vss. 29–30). Only if the
Christian leadership is equal to the task will the church be
saved. What are the specifics of this concern? The speech expresses a concern that the church leaders feed (shepherd) the
church (vs. 28), that they be alert to the dangers threatening
the church (vs. 31a), and that they avoid being subverted by
a love of money (vss. 33–35a). The farewell speech secondly
offers the basis for the expectations for the new generation's
leadership. It points to the obedience of the older generation.

On the one side, Paul is shown to have been obedient to his commission from the risen Lord (Acts 9:15–16): suffering (vs. 19) and testifying to both Jews and Greeks (vs. 21). On the other side, he is depicted as obedient to the words of the earthly Jesus (Luke 12:35–48; Acts 20:35b): he fed them (vss. 20, 27, 31) and he was not greedy (vss. 33–35a). The speech also points out the difference the older generation's obedience made. Acts portrays the apostolic age as a period free from heresy and schism (just as Hegesippus said it was—Eusebius, *Church History*, 3:32:7–8; see 4:22:4). This has the effect of saying that a minister's faithfulness does make a difference. Apostolic faithfulness to its commission is a model for each new generation of ministers to emulate. On our faithfulness depends the health and well being of the Lord's people.

A more general application of the farewell speech would focus on "Modelling the Faith." The use of Paul as a model here echoes a theme found elsewhere in Luke-Acts (see Luke 6:40; 8:16) and also in the Pauline letters (1 Cor 4:16; 11:1; Phil 3:17; 1 Thess 1:6; 2 Thess 3:7). The concern to have an *exempla* for the youth of the present to emulate instead of having to rely only on ancient models was also a concern of the pagan author Lucian and was why he wrote his *Life of Demonax*. The widespread recognition of the need to have someone to identify with is here utilized by the Third Evangelist in his portrayal of his hero, Paul.

The Christian's Gethsemane (21:1–16)

In the section, Acts 15:36—21:16, there are two parts: (1) 15:36—18:22, and (2) 18:23—21:16. Each of these parts ends on a similar note. (1) Acts 18:21 has Paul respond to the request that he stay longer in Ephesus, "I will return to you if God wills." This establishes the divine authority for the ministry in Ephesus to come in Acts 18:24—19:41. (2) Acts 21:13–14 has Paul respond to the prophecy about his impending imprisonment in Jerusalem (21:11), "I am ready not only to be imprisoned but even to die at Jerusalem for the name of the Lord Jesus" (see Acts 5:41; Rom 15:30–32) and the disciples say, "The will of the Lord be done." This shows that the events that overtake Paul in Jerusalem are a part of the divine plan. In other words, the basis in the divine will for each succeeding section is laid out at the end of the preceding one.

The various dimensions of this literary technique in the section, 18:23—21:16, needs more detailed investigation. First, in Acts 19:21 ("Paul resolved in the Spirit to . . . go to Jerusalem") and 20:22 ("I am going to Jerusalem bound in the Spirit") make it clear that Paul's going to Jerusalem is in obedience to the Holy Spirit's leading. Second, as he goes Paul is told by the Spirit (that is, in Christian prophecy) that imprisonment and affliction await him there (Acts 20:23; 21:4; 21:11). For example, Agabus in an act of prophetic symbolism takes the long cloth that was wound several times around Paul's waist to carry money and other things in (see Matt 10:9) and binds his own hands and feet. The accompanying word of interpretation spells out the future imprisonment of Paul. As in the case of Jesus (Luke 9:44; 18:32), the Jews will take him prisoner and deliver him into the hands of the Gentiles (Acts 21:11, echoing the language of the Third Gospel though actually in Acts the Romans rescue Paul from the hands of the Jews). Third, the function of Paul's knowing what to expect is to allow him and his companions to agree with God's will. If suffering and death are part of God's will, "The will of the Lord be done" (21:14). This, of course, echoes the scene on the Mount of Olives in Luke 22:39–46 where Jesus prays, "nevertheless not my will, but thine, be done." This is the Pauline Gethsemane! It shows, as does the case of Jesus in the Third Gospel, that suffering may be a part of the divine will for his servants, even though they be Spirit-empowered (Luke 3:21–22; 4:16–19; Acts 9:17). It shows, moreover, as does the case of Jesus in Luke, the Spirit-empowered person's submission to God's will, whatever it is. If it is to return to Ephesus, that is fine; if it is to be imprisoned and even die in Jerusalem, that must be done.

The clue to the Lukan perspective is found in the developmental treatment of Jesus' career in the Third Gospel. There Jesus' career falls into five stages: (1) dedication to God by his parents as an infant (Luke 2:22–24); (2) Jesus' personal agreement with the parental decisions when he reaches the age of accountability (Luke 2:41–52); (3) his empowering for ministry at age thirty (Luke 3:21–23); (4) his acceptance of rejection, suffering, and death as part of his way (Luke 9–23); and (5) resurrection, ascension, exaltation (Luke 24—Acts).

The Third Evangelist sees this prototypical development as defining the Christian Way. In Acts the two major components of the Way are echoed: that is, empowering (e.g., Acts 2) and suffering (e.g., Acts 14:22 and Paul's passion journey to Jerusalem which is parallel to that of Jesus in the Third Gospel). The components that are not reflected in Acts are missing because of their inappropriateness to the narrative (e.g., there is no need in Acts for an infancy narrative or for youthful commitment; there is no place for a resurrection that is still future). In Lukan thought, the disciple walks the Way of the pioneer of the faith (Acts 5:31, *archegos*). This includes the empowering and the subsequent suffering. If Lukan thought had defined the Christian way entirely in terms of empowering, it would have fallen into the pit of an over-realized eschatology (i.e., it would have claimed for the period between Jesus' resurrection and his second coming things that are appropriate only after the general resurrection—e.g., sinlessness; transcendence of sexuality; transcendence of sickness, suffering, and death; experience of a guaranteed affluence). If Luke-Acts had described the Christian way totally in terms of suffering, rejection, and death, it would have fallen into the abyss of an under-realized eschatology (i.e., it would not have claimed for the period between Jesus' resurrection and parousia all that is now available to believers in this period that is both now as well as not yet— e.g., the empowering presence of the Holy Spirit in an experience that is consciously known both to the person on whom the Spirit is poured out and to those witnessing the event; the occurrence of miracles through such empowered persons; the overwhelming success of the gospel in spite of every conceivable obstacle to it). The Third Evangelist falls prey to neither of these errors. He combines a strong "now" with a clear "not yet." This he makes clear in his narrative of the Acts which portrays Jesus disciples not only as baptized in the Holy Spirit but also as suffering and dying for the name of Jesus.

In the Lukan frame of reference suffering was not redemptive unless one had first experienced the divine empowering. Therefore, in the Lukan order of things, suffering is not a substitute for empowering but rather a component of the Christian way subsequent to empowering. One reason for this is that the experience of the Holy Spirit, seen prototypically in the career of the Lukan Jesus in Luke 3:21–22 (see Luke 4:16–21), combines a perception of two things: (1) that of being beloved of God ("You are my beloved Son"; the descent of the dove), and (2) that of being empowered by God ("The Spirit of the Lord is upon me"). From this derives the two things the followers of the way hold dear: (1) God is good, and (2) God is in control. Only after knowing this experientially can one undergo suffering profitably. Only then can one suffer and still affirm, in the face of one's overwhelming ignorance, that God is still in control and he is good. The Lukan Paul approaches his hard times believing God is in control (that is what the prophecy-fulfillment schema means) and willing to die if need be because he believes the Lord is good.

In Lukan thought that which enables a person to enter into suffering, without a loss of faith, is prayer (see Luke 18:1). So in the Third Gospel's narrative of Jesus' prayer on the Mount of Olives there is an inclusion: vss. 40 and 46, "Pray that you may not enter into temptation." In Acts, Paul is also depicted as kneeling in prayer in the face of his future suffering (Acts 20:36; 21:5), as Jesus did in Luke 22, even though the normal posture of prayer was standing (see Luke 18:11). The very posture is that of submission to the one he knows is both good and in control.

This passage offers a good opportunity to deal sermonically with the issue of "The Christian's Gethsemane," or the matter of "Suffering in Christian Life." Such a sermon based on this text would make two points. In the first place, it would point out that suffering is integral to the Christian way. Recognizing the fact of suffering in Christian experience and knowing its place and function can enable the Christian to agree with God's will in the matter and cooperate with his purposes. In the second place, the text points out that suffering is redemptive in the Christian way because of the Christian's experience of God both in the event of empowering (see Luke 3:21–22) and in the encounters of continuing prayer (see Luke 18:1–8). Christians approach suffering realistically and religiously: realistically, because suffering is a fact of human existence, Christians included; religiously, because it is only the Christians' experience of God that allows them to affirm in the midst of pain that God is both good and in control. To be able to affirm both in the face of suffering is the Christian distinctive.

The State in Christian Perspective (21:17—23:10)

Acts 21:17—23:10 is a thought unit dealing with Paul's testimony about Christ at Jerusalem (23:11a). The several dimensions of meaning to be found in the Lukan text may be grasped as this section's participation in various surface structures or patterns is probed. Multiple surface structures are a narrative's way of saying, "on the one hand, on the other," or "in the first place, in the second place, in the third place." That literature in antiquity was written with multiple patterns overlaid and crisscrossing one another was their way to guarantee that a text's meaning would not be reduced to one point only but would be allowed to say several things depending on how its organization was perceived.

(1) The first pattern controlling the development of this narrative section is a prophecy-fulfillment schema. In Luke-Acts this pattern is widespread. It is not too great an exaggeration to say that virtually everything in the Lukan narrative is a fulfillment of some type of prophecy (see Luke 1:1—"the things that have been fulfilled among us"). As prophecies of the OT, prophecies of living Jewish prophets, of Jesus, of early Christian prophets, and of angels find their fulfillment, the narrative flows along according to the divine plan. At the end of Acts the Evangelist's use of this device is especially prominent. The last two major units in Acts, 21:17—23:10 and 23:11—28:31, employ this schema as their dominant pattern. So in 20:23 and 21:11 the reader hears prophecies of Paul's impending imprisonment in Jerusalem. From 21:33, when Paul is bound with two chains, the prophecy's fulfillment is described. (That the prophecy comes in material that serves also as the conclusion to the previous thought unit merely reflects the Lukan use of the rhetorical principle verbalized by Lucian, *The Art of Writing History*, 55: "One thing should not only lie adjacent to the next, but be related to it and overlap at the edges.") When Luke uses this schema, it is his way of asserting the divine control of history. The will of the Lord is being done (21:14; 9:15–16) in spite

of human evil (see Rom 8:28; the Joseph stories in Genesis, especially Gen 50:20: "As for you, you meant evil against me; but God meant it for good, to bring it about that many people should be kept alive").

(2) The second surface structure related to this section is a recurring pattern in Acts: (a) outreach to the Gentiles; (b) legitimation of the outreach by Jerusalem; and (c) conciliatory actions to establish church unity taken by those involved in the Gentile mission (e.g., 10:1—11:18; 11:19–30; chaps. 13—15 and 16:1–4; chaps. 16—21). So 21:17–26 functions at the end of the missionary outreach in chapters 16—20 in the same way as 15:1–35 and 16:1–4 at the end of the journey in Acts 13—14. In each case, Paul returns to Jerusalem, where approval is given by the Jerusalem leadership to Paul on the principle of Gentile inclusion (15:1–35; 21:17–20a, 25). Then, once the principle is established, Paul takes conciliatory action (16:1–4; 21:20b–24, 26).

The Third Evangelist aims to legitimate the Gentile mission in this section as well as earlier. The Jerusalem Christians glorify God when they hear Paul relate the things God had done among the Gentiles through his ministry (21:19–20). They also reaffirm the original agreement to enable Gentile Christians to fellowship with practicing Jewish Christians (21:25). The speech of 22:1–21 says at two places that it was the risen Christ who had commissioned Paul for the Gentile mission. Vs. 15 has Ananias say that Paul had seen and heard Christ and would be "a witness for him to *all men*" (see Luke 2:31; 3:6; 24:47; Acts 2:17; 17:30). Vss. 18, 21 relate the message of the risen Christ to Paul, after his conversion while he is praying in the temple. "Depart, for I will send you far away to the Gentiles." This mission is tied to the fact that the Jews will not listen (see 13:46–47; 18:8–9; 28:25–28; see Luke 4:25–28). Just as the missionary outreach of Paul began with a heavenly vision (chap. 9), so it is framed on this side with an echo of the first appearance and a mention of one as yet unknown to the reader. Jesus himself stands behind the Gentile mission of Paul.

Once this principle is established, the Lukan Paul acts to allay the fears and suspicions of Christian Jews who have heard that he teaches "all the Jews who are among the Gentiles to forsake Moses, telling them not to circumcise their

children or observe the customs" (21:21). He acts in a way
that shows that he himself, a Christian Jew, lives in obser-
vance of the law (21:24). He underwrites the expenses of four
men under a vow, purifying himself along with them (vs. 24;
see 18:18b). The charges made against him by the Jews from
Asia (21:28) are shown to be false by his actions. They are
also denied by his speech in 22:1-21. There he portrays himself as a faithful Jew (vss. 1, 2, 3, 4-5, 17) who became a
Christian through the instrumentality of one Ananias, "a devout man according to the law, well spoken of by all the Jews
who lived" in Damascus (22:12), as well as through a heavenly vision (vss. 6-10). Furthermore, it was while he was praying in the temple that a second vision of the Lord gave him
his commission to go to the Gentiles (vss. 17-21). With word
and deed the Lukan Paul attests his faithfulness as a Jew. In
the Lukan scheme of things, this attempt to clarify his status
as a faithful Jew is his attempt to protect the unity of the one
church made up of Jews and Gentiles. The Lukan Paul is one
who acts out of a vision of the unity of the Christian community (see Eph 2:11-22; John 10:16). The Lukan Paul himself
lives in terms of Jewish mores, once the principle of a law-
free gospel for Gentiles is established, and permits other Jewish Christians to do the same. This is very much the position
taken in Justin Martyr, Dialogue with Trypho the Jew, 47.
Trypho, the Jew, asks Justin, the Christian, if Jews who are
converted to Christ but who wish to continue to observe the
law will be saved. Justin answers that they will, in his opin-
ion, so long as they do not try to make Gentiles do the same.

(3) The third pattern of organization is 21:17—23:11 is a
threefold repetition of material formally analogous to what
one finds in Mark 8:31—10:52: (a) 21:26-39; (b) 21:40—22:29;
(c) 22:30—23:10. In each of these three cycles of material one
is presented first with a situation in which Paul is acting with
reference to the Jews (Paul in the temple; Paul speaking to the
Jewish mob; Paul before the Sanhedrin), second with a clear
cut danger to Paul from Jewish violence ("away with him"—
21:36; "away with such a fellow from the earth. For he ought
not to live"—22:22; "the tribune, afraid that Paul would be
torn in pieces by them"—23:10a), and finally with his rescue
by Roman authorities ("he ordered him to be brought into the
barracks"—21:34; "The tribune commanded him to be

brought into the barracks"—22:24; "the tribune ... commanded the soldiers to go down and take him by force from among them and bring him into the barracks"—23:10b).

This pattern is connected with the recurring theme in Acts, that Roman rule is the Christians' best protection against mob violence (see 18:12-17; 19:23-41). When, at the end of the first cycle (21:37-39), Paul denies any connection with the revolutionary Egyptian (vs. 38; see Josephus, *War*, 2:13:5), the reader is brought into contact with yet another related theme. Christians, like their founder (Luke 2:1-7; 20:21-25), are respectfully obedient citizens (see Rom 13:1-7; 1 Tim 2:1-3; 1 Pet 2:13-17; Justin Martyr, *I Apology*, 17) who do not advocate revolutionary violence. When, at the end of the second cycle (22:24-29), Paul appeals to his Roman citizenship as a protection against examination by torture, there is yet another Lukan theme recurring. Christians have apostolic example to legitimate their use of their legal rights as a protection against injustice (see 16:37-39).

This passage may be preached in several ways depending on which way it is read. If one reads it primarily in terms of the prophecy-fulfillment pattern, then the sermon would focus on the sovereignty of God. The sermon could be developed using Genesis 50:20 as a complement to the Acts passage. The thrust of the message would be that, in spite of human evil, God works out his plan to give life to his creatures.

If one reads Acts 21:17—23:10 in terms of the second pattern developed previously, the thrust of the sermon would be on (1) reaching all people, and (2) keeping all those reached together, one in Christ's community. A title that would capture these two emphases would be "Universalism and Unity in Christ." Relevant parallel material is found not only in Eph 2:11-22 but also in I Cor 8:9 and Rom 14:19 and 15:1-2.

If one reads the passage in terms of the three parallel cycles of 21:26-39; 21:40—22:29; and 22:30—23:10, then the sermon would focus on "The State in Christian Perspective." Such a sermon might deal first with the fact that the state's order is a protection for Christians against the dangers of anarchy. It would then need to deal with the implications of that fact. First, Christians do not advocate revolutionary violence to overthrow the state. Second, Christians do use their legal rights as a remedy for injustice at the hands of the state. Viewed in this way, the narrative gives Christians an apostolic (14:4, 14) precedent for a certain way of viewing and relating to the state.

Giving an Account for the Hope That Is in You (23:11—26:32)

Acts 23:11—26:32 is the first of two parts of the larger section, 23:11—28:31. The larger section is built, like the previous one, around a prophecy-fulfillment pattern. In 23:11 ("as you have testified about me at Jerusalem, so you must bear witness also at Rome") and 27:24 ("you must stand before Caesar"), there are two prophecies, one by the risen Christ and the other by an angel of God, of Paul's witness in Rome before Caesar. In 28:14b–31 there is the fulfillment.

Acts 23:12—26:32 is a coherent thought unit with a carefully wrought surface structure. There are three cycles of material built out of the same five components. The first cycle looks like this.

> A—Plot to kill Paul (23:12–16)
> B—Paul's action to protect himself (23:17–25)
> C—Official verdict about Paul (23:26–30)
> D—Caesarean hearings (1)
> 1. The charges of the Jews (24:1–9)
> 2. The Pauline defense (24:10–21)
> E—Governor Felix's failings (24:24–27)

The second cycle contains the same five components in a different order.

> A—Plot to kill Paul (25:1–3)
> D—Caesarean hearings (2) (25:4–8)
> 1. The charges of the Jews (25:7)
> 2. The Pauline defense (25:8)
> E—Governor Festus' failings (25:9)
> B—Paul's action to protect himself (25:10–12)
> C—Official verdict about Paul (25:13–21)

The third cycle contains only the two core components out of these five.

> D—Caesarean hearings (3) (25:22–26:23)
> 1. The charges of the Jews (25:24)
> 2. The Pauline defense (26:1–23)
> C—Official verdict about Paul (26:24–32)

A reading of the narrative must focus on these components in order to grasp the Lukan intent.

(1) The main point of 23:12—26:32 is found in the official verdict. Paul is declared innocent by human authority of any crime for which the State is responsible: the tribune, Claudius Lysias (23:29), the governor Felix by implication (24:23, 26, 27), the governor Festus (25:25), and the Jewish king, Agrippa (26:32). The matter at issue concerns inner-Jewish religious debates (23:29; 25:18), in particular, the claim that Jesus who was dead, is now alive (25:19b; 26:23). This is the specific implication of Paul's claim that the issue in his imprisonment is his hope of the resurrection from the dead (26:6; 24:15, 21; see 23:6). All of this has the effect of saying that Paul (Christianity by implication) is guilty of treason neither against Rome nor against Judaism. Luke has used the Roman officials and a Jewish king as witnesses for the defense. In making this point, the Evangelist is not addressing the world or the synagogue; he is speaking to Christians (see Luke 1:1—"the things fulfilled among us"). In so doing he is concerned to shape Christian identity. This, he says, is the way apostolic Christianity sees itself: as a branch of Judaism that believes in the resurrection and that is politically responsible.

(2) The other components all relate in one way or another to the matter of suffering and abuse endured by Christians (see Heb 10:32–34; 1 Pet 4:4 for the ongoing experience). Component B, Paul's action to protect himself, speaks to the matter of how to act when threatened with the loss of life by senseless violence. Do not rush into martyrdom; use your legal options. The Lukan Paul makes use of the Roman system to preserve his life (23:17–22; 25:10–12; see 16:37–39). In so doing Paul's behavior corresponds to that of Jesus in the Third Gospel, not only in their four trials each (Jesus: Luke 22:66–71; 23:1–5; 23:6–12; 23:13–25; Paul: Acts 23:1–10; 24:1–21; 25:8; 26:1–23) but also in their lack of any lust for death (Jesus: Luke 22:42—"Father, if thou art willing, remove this cup from me"). Although both Jesus and Paul were willing to die, if that was God's will (Luke 22:42; Acts 21:13), neither sought martyrdom as Ignatius of Antioch, the young Origen, and others did (see my Reading Luke, pp. 215–16). Again the narrative aims to shape Christian identity. Chris-

tians may die as martyrs but this should only happen after
they have exhausted every legal avenue of recourse. Martyrdom is not suicide.

The narrative also makes very clear what Christians are
and are not to expect from the State. On the one hand, the
State is available to offer the Christians protection against
violence (23:17–22). The State respects a Christian's Roman
citizenship (22:27–29; 25:16), often sparing no expense to
guarantee his physical safety (23:23—200 soldiers, 70 horse-
men, 200 spearmen). On the other hand, one must be realistic
about what can be expected in the way of the implementation of Roman justice. If Paul is deemed completely innocent,
why does he remain a prisoner? At one level, Paul's continuing imprisonment is viewed as due to human evil. Both Felix
(24:27) and Festus (25:9) diluted the justice due Paul by their
desire to please the Jews (see 12:3). Moreover, Felix's desire
for a bribe (24:26) gives him an additional reason to keep
Paul in prison. Even though Roman officials recognize his innocence, they do not give Paul full justice because of their
own personal failings. Whereas the Christian may expect to
benefit from Roman justice contingent on the character of
the individual administrators, there is one area in which
Christians should not expect anything from the State. The
Roman State is not competent to decide the religious or theological matters about which Jews and Christians clash (Acts
25:20a, 26; 26:24; see 18:15). The matter of the resurrection is
incomprehensible to the State.

Component D—2, the Pauline defense, focuses on the Christian use of persecution as an opportunity to further the Christian cause. Paul's imprisonment is the means by which God's
will is accomplished. First, he can thereby fulfill his commission given in Acts 9:15: "to carry my name before the Gentiles and *kings* and the sons of Israel." Second, it gives him an
opportunity to obey the words of Jesus in Luke 21:12–13:
"they will lay hands on you and persecute you, delivering
you up to the synagogues and *prisons*, and you will be
brought *before kings and governors* for my name's sake. This
will be a time for testimony." A time of persecution is a moment of opportunity to bear witness.

In his speeches in these chapters—more witness than defense—Paul's basic technique is personal testimony. Acts

26:1–23 is representative. After the conventional section in which he flatters the judge (26:2–3), Paul's speech is testimony. (a) He lived as a Pharisee, believing in the resurrection from the dead (vss. 4–8). (b) He was a persecutor of the church (vss. 9–11; see 1 Tim 1:13). (c) His life was radically changed, however, by a heavenly vision (vss. 12–18; see 23:9). (d) His present behavior is in obedience to the heavenly vision (vss. 19–22a). This behavior arising from his religious experience on the Damascus road is in continuity with the prophets and Moses (vss. 22b–23) and echoes the risen Jesus' own interpretation of the Scriptures (with vs. 23, see Luke 24:25–27, 45–47).

In Luke-Acts there are two types of witnesses: those who were with him throughout his earthly existence and those who were not continually with Jesus during his lifetime. The former include those like the Twelve who were with him from the baptism of John until the ascension (Acts 1:21–22). The latter are those who have experienced the power and grace of the Lord and bear witness to what he has done for them (see Luke 8:38–29). Paul belongs to this latter group. He bears witness to his personal experience. The risen Christ says to him: "I have appeared to you for this purpose, to appoint you to serve and bear witness to the things in which you have seen me and to those in which I will appear to you" (26:16). For the Lukan Paul, testimony to the ongoing experience of the risen Lord will be his unanswerable argument. At the same time, Luke makes clear that it is not just any experience of the numinous but one that stands in continuity with Jesus and with Scripture (see my *Reading Luke*, pp. 99–101). From the Third Evangelist's point of view, it is only when the knowledge of the tradition is made alive by personal experience that an effective witness can be made. The tradition may evoke the experience and it may correct the experience, but it is no substitute for the experience. When the Lukan Paul bears witness, it is to his religious experience and out of that experience. This is its power.

This narrative section contains a number of sermonic options. One possibility would build on the unit's focus on Paul's defense. 1 Peter 4:15b says: "Always be prepared to make a defense to any one who calls you to account for the hope that is in you; yet do it with gentleness and reverence."

Col 4:6 says: "Let your speech always be gracious, seasoned with salt, so that you may know how you ought to answer every one." Acts 23—26 sets forth the factors that contribute to a Christian's ability to testify to his/her faith. The factors are two. On the one hand, the Christian needs to know God. Paul did not know only about God. He knew God. This living experience was the basis for his effective testimony. It was an experience in continuity with Jesus and with Scripture, but Scripture and a knowledge of the earthly Jesus did not substitute for the experience of the risen Christ. On the other hand, the Christian who would bear an effective testimony needs to know who he/she is. Paul not only had a living religious experience, but he also knew how that experience fit into the history of a specific religious community and how that community and experience were related to the cultural-political environment in which he lived. In this sense, he understood who he was. It was this combination of living religious experience and knowledge of its history and context that made Paul a model for Christians who were being called upon to give an account for their hope. It is no different today when we are "Giving an Account for the Hope That Is in You."

The preacher should probably refine the sermon outline in the previous section on "The State in Christian Perspective" in light of the additional information supplied by Luke in this unit.

Stormy Weather (27:1—28:31)

Acts 27:1—28:31 is the final section of the two volume Lukan work. It consists of three scenes: (1) 27:1–44 and 28:11–14, a sea journey to Rome interrupted by storm and shipwreck (see Luke 8:40–42, 49–56, one story interrupted by another, 8:43–48); (2) 28:1–10, two episodes on land after deliverance from the sea; and (3) 28:15–31, Paul in Rome. Each scene must be examined in turn.

(1) Scene One (27:1–44 and 28:11–14) is controlled by two prophecies of Paul and their fulfillment. The first is found in 27:9–10. The background for the prophecy is a reference to the time of the year: "because the fast (the Jewish Day of Atonement, September–October) had already gone by" (vs. 9). This is important because after mid-September sailing

was doubtful and after early November impossible. This has the effect of saying that the cause of the storm was the time of year. Paul's prophecy is twofold: there will be (a) a loss of the ship and its cargo, and (b) a loss of lives (vs. 10). This prophecy is only partially fulfilled. In 27:18 cargo is cast overboard, as also in 27:38 ("throwing out the wheat into the sea"); in 27:41 the ship breaks up in the surf. The predicted loss of lives is averted, however, by a second prophecy of Paul: "there will be no loss of life among you, but only of the ship" (vs. 22; see vs. 34). In 27:44 this is fulfilled when "all escaped to land." Unlike Jonah whose presence endangered lives on ship, Paul's presence is the avenue of salvation for those on board. The second prophecy has yet another component. The angel of God says to Paul: "Do not be afraid, Paul; you must stand before Caesar" (vs. 24). This is fulfilled in the narrative when the sea voyage is finally completed and Paul comes to Rome (28:14). This makes it very clear that the security of Paul, and by extension those with him, is due to God's intervention. Looked at as a whole, the narrative says the storm was due to the time of the year, the deliverance to God's determination that Paul reach Rome (fulfilling Acts 23:11 and 1:8).

(2) Scene Two (28:1–10) consists of two episodes on land after escape from the sea. In the first one (28:1–6), Paul is bitten by a viper. This brings a certain response from the natives of Malta. "No doubt this man is a murderer. Though he has escaped from the sea, justice has not allowed him to live" (28:4). When Paul's death did not occur as expected, they thought him a god (see 14:15).

At this point it is necessary to turn to some background materials for assistance in understanding the significance of the storm-shipwreck and the snake bite stories. The background is the Mediterranean belief that divine forces in cooperation with nature (especially storms at sea) and the animal kingdom (especially snakes) punish wickedness. Examples from the Greco-Roman world are numerous. (a) Homer, *Odyssey*, 12:127–41, 259–446, tells how Odysseus' crew were destroyed in a shipwreck because they had killed Helios' sacred cattle. (b) Chariton's novel attests the conviction that the polluted are drowned at sea while the just are delivered (3:3:10; 3:3:18; 3:4:9–10). (c) Lucian, *Peregrinus*, 42–44, criticizes

Peregrinus' fear in the face of a storm at sea as proof that he was a charlatan. (d) So certain was such punishment from the sea believed to be that in certain circumstances the absence of destruction by storm could be adduced as proof of innocence. Antiphon's *Murder of Herodes*, 82–83, argues that his client, Helion, is innocent because on all his sea journeys he has enjoyed safety. (see G.B. Miles and G. Trompf, "Luke and Antiphon: The Theology of Acts 27—28 in the Light of Pagan Beliefs About Divine Retribution, Pollution, and Shipwreck," *Harvard Theological Review*, 69 [1976], pp. 259–67; D. Ladonceur, "Hellenistic Preconceptions of Shipwreck and Pollution as a Context for Acts 27—28," *Harvard Theological Review*, 73 [1980], pp. 435–49, argues that Andocides' speech in *De Mysteriis*, 137–39, is a better example than that of Antiphon.) If the divine justice administered by storm and shipwreck fail, then the animal kingdom stands ready to assist. An epitaph by Statyllus Flaccus on a shipwrecked seaman killed by snake bite concludes: "Why did he struggle against the waves? He did not escape the lot which was destined for him on land" (E. Haenchen, *The Acts of the Apostles* [Philadelphia: Westminster Press, 1971], p. 713, n.5).

The Jewish world also knew the convention in both biblical and post-biblical times. (a) In Jonah 1:4 a storm comes in response to the prophet's disobedience (1:7–10). Only when he is thrown out into the sea does the storm subside (1:12, 15). (b) In the Babylonian Talmud, *Baba Mezia* 58b–59, one hears that after the excommunication of Rabbi Eliezer, Rabbi Gamaliel was travelling in a ship. A huge wave arose to drown him. He cried out to God that he was innocent and at that the raging sea subsided. (c) In the Tosefta, *Sanhedrin* 8:3, Rabbi Simeon ben Shetah says he saw a man running after a fellow into a deserted building. When Simeon entered, he saw the one slain and the other dripping blood. "But he who knows the thoughts, he exacts vengeance from the guilty; for the murderer did not stir from the place before a serpent bit him so that he died." (d) In the Jerusalem Talmud, *Berakoth* 5:1, one hears that once when Rabbi Haninah ben Dosa was praying, he was bitten by a snake. It not only did not interrupt his prayer but later the snake was found dead at the entrance to its den. Whether it was Jew or Greek, the Mediterranean populace believed that nature and the animal kingdom cooperated with divine power to punish the wicked.

That Paul was not the cause of the storm and shipwreck (the time of year was—27:9) but rather the means of the travelers' deliverance (27:21–25, 34) is Luke's way to say he is pronounced innocent by God. That Paul was bitten by a viper and survived is the author's way to affirm that Paul is a righteous man (see Luke 10:19). If chapters 23—26 have as their main thrust that human authorities pronounce Paul innocent, these two stories in Acts 27—28 affirm that God does also.

The second episode in Scene Two is a healing story (28:7–10). The father of Publius, the chief man on the island, was sick with fever and dysentery (see Luke 4:38–40). "Paul visited him and prayed, and putting his hands on him healed him" (vs. 8). The point of this healing in its Lukan context is again the righteous status of Paul. James 5:16b–18 puts it succinctly. "The prayer of a righteous man has great power in its effects. Elijah was a man of like nature with ourselves and he prayed fervently that it might not rain; and for three years and six months it did not rain on the earth. Then he prayed again and the heaven gave rain, and the earth brought forth its fruit." Paul's prayer for healing is effective because Paul is a righteous man. The three episodes of Scenes One and Two, therefore, say the same thing. Paul's innocence-righteousness (Luke 23:47) is attested by God.

(3) Scene Three (28:15–31), Paul in Rome, is held together by an inclusion (vs. 16—"Paul was allowed to stay by himself, with the soldier that guarded him"; vs. 30—"And he lived there two whole years at his own expense"). The three parts of the Roman episode need attention (vss. 15–16; 17–28; 30–31). (a) Vs. 15 tells how Christian brethren from Rome travel some forty miles to the Forum of Appius and some thirty miles to Three Taverns to greet Paul. This could only be if Paul was regarded by them as an important figure. Note that the reference is to brethren not churches. Elsewhere (18:24–28; 19:1–7) when Luke speaks in this way, it is because he both wants to recognize the existence of Christianity prior to Paul in that locale and wants to portray Pauline Christianity as the norm for that place. The Lukan Paul is

an important person for Roman Christians and one who completes the Christian movement in the city.

(b) Vss. 17–28 consist of two episodes, each with its speech by Paul. In vss. 17–22, the first, there is a gathering of the Jews, Paul makes a speech, and the Jews respond. The speech here is a personal defense (vss. 17b–20), similar to those in chapters 22, 23, 24, 26. Paul portrays himself as a devout Jew, mistreated by his countrymen, who is in bonds because of the hope of Israel (see 23:6; 24:15; 26:7). He is a man faithful to his ancestral religion, as a righteous man should be. In vss. 23–28, the second episode, there is another gathering of Jews, after Paul preaches and the Jewish response is made, Paul gives a speech (vss. 25–28). This speech is a defense of his turning to the Gentiles (see 13:46–47; 18:6; 19:8–9). Jewish rejection forces him to it. This word about his turning to the Gentiles because of Jewish rejection, like the earlier statements (13:46–7; 18:6) and practice (19:8–10) often leads readers to suppose that Paul will never again speak to Jews. Yet in 14:1, in 18:8, 19, and in 19:10, he does precisely that. It is the same with Acts 28. The purpose of these three statements about turning to Gentiles is not to indicate an end to any efforts to win Jews but to explain why the church in Antioch, Corinth, Ephesus, and Rome is predominantly Gentile. Luke's answer is that the dominant Gentile composition of these Pauline churches is due to Jewish rejection of the gospel.

(c) Vss. 30–31 tell the reader that Paul's work in Rome was long (two years; see 18:11; 19:10, that is, especially blessed) and unhindered (that is, tolerated by Rome; see also 27:3, 43). This ending of Acts is functionally similar to 2 Kings 25:27–30 and Jer 52:31–34. Just as the Deuteronomist and Jeremiah end their works on an optimistic note (in the exile the Davidic king is given relative freedom) to presage better things to come, so the Third Evangelist looks to a brighter future, presaged by the relative freedom of the prisoner Paul in Rome. Paul's Roman circumstances are both a fulfillment of the prophecy of Acts 1:8 and a sign of more success for the gospel yet to come. See G. W. Trompf, "On Why Luke Declined to Recount the Death of Paul: Acts 27—28 and Beyond," in *Luke—Acts: New Perspectives from the Society of Biblical Literature Seminar* [New York: Crossroad, 1983], pp. 225–39.)

A couple of sermon ideas come to mind out of this passage. One might be called "Making the Most of the Time" (Eph 5:16//Col 4:5). It would focus on Paul's ability to be a witness to his Lord in whatever circumstances he found himself. Paul was able to see an opportunity to witness to Jesus in unscheduled times and places (28:1–10). He was also able to seize the opportunity to witness in disadvantageous times and places (28:30–31).

Another sermon possibility based on this text would be "Stormy Weather," a circumstance everyone has either just come out of, is now in, or will be in eventually. When your enemies oppress you, when your circumstances depress you, and when the vessel of your life is threatened with shipwreck, what can you as a Christian do? The Lukan Paul is our model. His life story teaches us first that you cannot depend on human resources. Others can offer only partial acceptance (see 27:1, 3, 42; 28:21–22, 24). Others can profer only limited assistance (see 27:18–19, 32, 38, 40; 28:2, 10, 15). Paul's story teaches us secondly that you can depend on God. He will attest your innocence, accepting you totally. He will give you adequate assistance, preserving your life, answering your prayers, and bringing you safely to the fulfillment of his purpose for your life. When stormy weather comes, rely on the one who made you, who bought you, and who is with you to the end.

Bibliography

Two commentaries are recommended to be read in connection with each other: Ernest Haenchen, *The Acts of the Apostles* (Philadelphia: Westminster Press, 1971) and I. Howard Marshall, *The Acts of the Apostles* (Grand Rapids: Wm. B. Eerdman, 1980).

Three volumes of essays offer real assistance to the student of Acts: F. J. Foakes Jackson and Kirsopp Lake, *The Beginnings of Christianity: The Acts of the Apostles, Vol. V: Additional Notes* (Grand Rapids: Baker Book House reprint, 1966), Charles H. Talbert (ed.), *Perspectives on Luke–Acts* (Danville, VA: National Association of Baptist Professors of Religion, 1978; now distributed by Mercer University Press, Macon, GA 31207), and Charles H. Talbert (ed.), *Luke-Acts: New Perspectives from the Society of Biblical Literature Seminar* (New York: Crossroad Publishing Company, 1983).

One monograph offers special help in certain Lukan themes in Acts: Jacob Jervell, *Luke and the People of God: A New Look at Luke–Acts* (Minneapolis: Augsburg Publishing House, 1972).

A variety of types of spirituality are found in the New Testament. For help in making sense of the particular form in Acts, several books are valuable. Morton T. Kelsey, *God, Dreams and Revelation* (Minneapolis: Augsburg Publishing House, 1974), is helpful on visions. Morton T. Kelsey, *Healing and Christianty* (San Francisco: Harper & Row, 1973), gives assistance on healing miracles. Morton T. Kelsey, *Tongue Speaking* (New York: Crossroad, 1981), interprets the meaning of glossalalia. Matthew and Dennis Linn (eds.), *Deliverance Prayer* (Ramsey, N.J.: Paulist Press, 1981), offer a series of articles dealing with prayers of exorcism. J. Panagopoulos (ed.), *Prophetic Vocation in the New Testament and Today* (Leiden: Brill, 1977), presents a collection of essays on the nature of prophecy in early Christianity and today.

One article is particularly helpful in grasping the developmental character of the Lukan "Way." This is Charles H. Talbert, "The Way of the Lukan Jesus: Dimensions of Lukan Spirituality," *Perspectives in Religious Studies*, 9 (1982), pp. 237–50.